The Janáček Opera Libretti Translations and Pronunciation

Volume I
Příhody lišky Bystroušky
The Cunning Little Vixen

Timothy Cheek

The Scarecrow Press, Inc.
Lanham, Maryland, and Oxford
2003

SCARECROW PRESS, INC.

Published in the United States of America
by Scarecrow Press, Inc.
A Member of the Rowman & Littlefield Publishing Group
4501 Forbes Boulevard, Lanham, Maryland 20706
www.scarecrowpress.com

PO Box 317
Oxford
OX2 9RU, UK

British Library Cataloguing in Publication Information Available

Library of Congress Cataloging-in-Publication Data

Janâaécek, Leoés, 1854-1928.
  [Operas. Librettos. English & Czech]
  The Janacek opera libretti : translations and pronunciation / Timothy
Cheek.
    p. cm.
  Includes bibliographical references and index.
  ISBN 0-8108-4671-3 (cloth : alk. paper)
  1. Janâaécek, Leoés, 1854–1928. Operas. 2. Operas—Librettos. I.
Cheek, Timothy, 1957– II. Title.
ML49.J36 J37 2003
782.1'0268—dc21   2002153032

Dirigentovi Bohumilovi Gregoru

Contents

Preface

Much has changed since the time Leoš Janáček sought the support of the writer Max Brod, who translated many of his libretti from Czech into German and opened the door to international exposure. Now, thanks largely to supertitles, audiences expect more and more to hear opera in its original language, and this at a time when the operas of Janáček are more firmly established than ever before in the repertory of opera houses worldwide.

For their vocal works, composers begin with words alone. Singers and those who perform with them should do the same. For Czech composers, the Czech language went beyond a basic means of communication to a symbol of Czech identity when, after well over a hundred years of domination by the Hapsburgs, their language was formally banned and came close to extinction. Under various reforms the language was coaxed back into "legitimacy" during the nineteenth century, and wonderful Czech poets and writers appeared. These were soon followed by composers who would meld music and word into the great art forms of opera and song, most notably under Smetana and Dvořák. With Janáček, the Czech language and music truly find a match, as this composer sought to capture the natural, emotional inflection of every character's utterance. The care, attention, and respect that every great artist gives to the words in vocal works in English, French, German, Italian, Russian, etc., must also be given to the great Czech works. The rewards of communicating the nuances of this expressive language and of forging the link between the words and the music are truly immense.

The present volume is the first in a series on Janáček's opera libretti. The author hopes it will stand alongside Nico

Castel's invaluable volumes on Italian libretti, offering assistance to non-Czech singers, those who coach and conduct them, stage directors, and passionate listeners.

The order of this series is not chronological but follows closely behind the finishing touches of any recently revised editions made by Dr. John Tyrrell, Sir Charles Mackerras, or Jiří Zahrádka; it also takes into account the most popular of Janáček's operas. Volume two, for example, will be *Kát'a Kabanová*, an opera that has been fully revised with every *ě* and *ř* accounted for. *Jenůfa* will contain the words to both the Kovařovic version and the revised Brno version. With *Příhody lišky Bystroušky* there are no revisions planned in the foreseeable future. It is also the one Janáček opera most likely to be performed in a university setting as well as by a professional company; in that sense it is the most accessible. This book, then, is based on the orchestral score UE 7566 of 1924 and the piano/vocal score UE 7564 of 1924 (which is now actually the second edition of 1925). It is often difficult to make out some of the Czech diacritical marks and punctuation, some of which are missing altogether; there are some misprints (and even a missing word). As a result the careful editing of the present volume should benefit all those involved in mounting a production or studying the work. Further, the author has made comparisons to the original novel by Rudolf Těsnohlídek on which the libretto is based. For those who would like to read the novel in English, there is one existing translation, which is excellent (Těsnohlídek 1985). Certain stylistic, musical, and cultural matters have also been addressed to better illuminate Janáček's unique voice. As with the author's book *Singing in Czech*, it is hoped that this series will help open more doors to moving performances of these great works.

Acknowledgments

Besides the exemplary input and editing from the staff at Scarecrow Press, a book like this one requires another set of critical eyes, well versed in the International Phonetic Alphabet as it applies to Czech diction, to detect any typographical errors among the many detailed IPA symbols. For this I am grateful to Milena Grubor, who caught some wayward errors before they could be set in stone. Absolutely essential, too, was someone well-acquainted with Moravian dialect who could both edit my translations and shed light on slang and cultural matters. For this I was extremely fortunate to have the assistance of Professor Zdenka Brodská, lecturer in Czechoslovakian literature at the University of Michigan, a native of Brno, Moravia, and a very knowledgeable admirer of Janáček's operas. Musically I am indebted to the teaching of conductor Bohumil Gregor with whom I carried out an apprenticeship at the National Theater, Prague, on this very opera in 1995. Besides his conducting, his great attention to the words in coaching sessions was truly inspiring. I am happy that he accepted the dedication of this book while, it so happens, he was preparing yet another new production of *Příhody lišky Bystroušky* at the National Theatre for the fall of 2002 and battling the aftermath of the terrible floods of that summer. Many thanks to Dr. John Tyrrell for his endorsement, support, and invaluable criticisms, especially given his very busy schedule. Thanks, too, to my wife Bohuslava Jelínková—a stellar *vážka* in the same 1995 production—above all for all your support! Much thanks, of course, go to European American Music Distributors, LLC, and Universal Edition for permission to reprint Janáček's libretto; and to Ctibor Lolek, for permission to reprint some of the illustrations made by his father, Stanislav Lolek—drawings that were the inspiration for the novel that so sparked the imagination of Janáček.

Introduction

Pronunciation

International Phonetic Alphabet (IPA)

The reader is referred to the author's book *Singing in Czech: A Guide to Czech Lyric Diction and Vocal Repertoire*, with a foreword by Sir Charles Mackerras (Scarecrow Press, 2001). This work includes a CD where all the Czech sounds, IPA symbols, and other details are fully exlained and demonstrated. Although this book uses IPA, the Czech language is so phonetic that after study many will find it necessary for only certain details. Keep in mind the following, and also see the "Pronunciation Checklist" in Appendix A for common mistakes by English-speaking singers:

(1) The Czech [a] and all other vowels are bright, much like Italian. Czech is the brightest of all the Slavic languages and contrasts greatly with Russian in overall sound.

(2) There is no closed [e] sound in Czech, only its open [ɛ] counterpart.

(3) The open [ɪ] represents a sound that is only a shade more open than the very closed Czech [iː]. It sits high and bright.

(4) The Czech consonants are forward and unaspirated, much like Italian.

(5) The sounds [n], [d], and [t] must be softened before the letter *i* or *í*. This book uses the following symbols for these

1

three soft consonants:

$$[ɲ] \quad [d'] \quad [t']$$

The more precise IPA for these three sounds is:

$$[ɲ] \quad [ɟ] \quad [c]$$

This author, as explained in *Singing in Czech*, has chosen to use [d'] and [t'] because they are the preferred symbols used by Czech linguists and are easier to equate with the sounds they represent. For those singers who have sung in Russian, note that these Czech palatal sounds are different from Russian palatal*ized* consonants in sound and in formation—all three Czech sounds being formed with the tip of the tongue touching the bottom teeth. Czech has no palatalized consonants. To be especially avoided is the substitution of [nj], [dj], and [tj] for these sounds.

(6) The pronunciation of the Czech written *ř* is shown as follows:

[ř] in this book represents the voiced sound

[Ř] in this book represents the unvoiced sound

Remember that although [ř] is often described as the simultaneous pronunciation of rolled [rr] and [ʒ] (and for the unvoiced [Ř] of an *un*voiced rolled [rr] and [ʃ]), it is only *one* sound. For example, the word *moře* [sea] must *not* sound like *morže*. Remember, too, that the position from which to learn this sound is a smile, not rounded lips.

Both sounds are fully explained and demonstrated by native Czech singers in *Singing in Czech*, along with exercises (Cheek 2001, 66–70).

(7) The symbol [ʔ] represents a glottal.

(8) The Czech sound [ɦ], as opposed to the English [h], represents a voiced sound, one that *always* has a pitch. (It is nothing like [x]!)

(9) Czech stress is always on the first syllable, except for prepositions and their objects. In those cases, the preposition takes over the initial stress, and the two words are pronounced as one. In the IPA, this is shown with a slur:

[za‿t'iːm]
za tím
behind it

Za tím, then, is pronounced as if it were written *zatím*, with the stress on *za*. The slur is shown in the IPA even if there is a glottal, as in *v okně* [f‿ʔɔkɲɛ] (in the window).

(10) Length in Czech is a separate issue from stress. Long vowels are clearly marked by the *čárka*, what looks like an accent mark, over the vowel. The IPA used to indicate length is a colon after the long sound:

[janaːt͡ʃɛk]
Janáček

In Janáček's name, the stress is on the short first syllable, followed by a long unstressed syllable and a short final syllable. The letter *u* can have a *čárka* or a *kroužek* (little circle) over its long version, as in *krůta* (turkey).

See chapter five of *Singing in Czech* for this essential element of Czech inflection. Holding a vowel too long can change the grammatical function of a word, alter its meaning completely, or even make it unintelligible.

(11) The combination *mě*, by itself or anywhere in a word, must be pronounced as [mɲɛ], as if the spelling were *mně*.

(12) Double consonants, when performed similar to Italian,

are shown with a colon in the IPA:

[jɛn ː nɛbudɛli]
jen   nebudeli

Otherwise, the sounds are rearticulated. Many cases are debatable, of course. (See "Double Consonants" in *Singing in Czech*.)

(13) The Czech [x] is not as far back as the German [x], nor as far forward as the German [ç]. Czech linguists use the symbol [x] to represent their sound that is in between the two German ones.

In the following chart the IPA is in quasi-alphabetical order, since it is the IPA that the majority of readers will be referring to the most in this book.

IPA	Czech	Nearest equivalent
[a]	a	Italian *fantasma*
[aː]	á	(The same, long)
[b]	b, p	Italian *bambino*
[d]	d, t	(Almost dental) Italian *dove*
[d']	d, d', d̆, t, t', t̆	See (5) above; absolutely NOT [dj]
[d͡ʒ]	dž, č	Italian *giubilare*
[d͡z]	c	English *fads*, Italian *zero*
		(The letter *c* is only occasionally voiced, as in *leckdo* [many a person] [lɛd͡zgdɔ])
[ɛ]	e	Italian *celeste*
[ɛː]	é	(The same, long)
[f]	f, v	English *frank*
[g]	g, k	Spanish *gato*
[ɦ]	h, ch	Close to the English exclamation *Heavens!*
[ɪ]	i, y	German *ich*
[iː]	í, ý	Italian *vino*
[j]	j	Like English *yes*, but clearer, more distinct
		(See Cheek 2001, 20-21 for other instances of the [j] sound)

[ⁱ]	j	The same, but as a glide to a consonant or as an off-glide, as in the French *soleil* [sɔlɛːⁱ]
[k]	k, g	Spanish *comer*
[l]	l	(Almost dental) Italian *liquido*
[ḷ]	l	The same, but vocalic (with no preceding *schwa*!)
[m]	m	English *music*
[n]	n	(Almost dental) Italian *naso*
[ɲ]	ň, n (mě)	(Never [nj]!) Italian *ogni*
[ŋ]	n	Further back than English *drink*, *sing*
[ɔ]	o	British *hot*
[ɔː]	ó	(The same, long)
[p]	p, b	Italian *prego*
[r]	r	Italian *caro*
[ṛ]	r	Vocalic rolled *r*; unlike [ḷ], it can begin with a *schwa* if the note is relatively long
[rr]	r	Italian *carro*
[ř]	ř	See (6) above. No equivalents, voiced
[Ř]	ř	See (6) above. No equivalents, unvoiced
[s]	s, z	Italian *sono*
[ss]	s	Italian *posso*
[ʃ]	š, ž	German *Schule*
[t]	t, d	(Almost dental) Italian *tenere*
[t']	t, t', ťˇ, d, d', ďˇ	See (5) above; absolutely NOT [tj]
[t͡s]	c	English *cats*, German *zu*
[t͡ʃ]	č	Brighter than English *cheek*
[u]	u	Similar to English *pool*
[uː]	ú, ů (The same, long, and only slightly more closed)
[v]	v, f	Italian *vino*
[x]	ch, h	In between German *ich* and *ach*
[ɣ]	ch, h	The same but voiced, as in Spanish *agua*
[z]	z, s	Italian *casa*
[ʒ]	ž, š	French *je*
[ʔ]		Glottal

Moravian Dialect

The Czech Republic consists of two main regions, Bohemia to the west and Moravia to the east. The main city of
Moravia is Brno, and the main city of Bohemia is Prague
(Praha), also the capital of the entire country. Janáček was
from Moravia, and many of his vocal works are in Moravian
dialect, including *Příhody lišky Bystroušky* [The adventures of
the vixen Bystrouška; The cunning little vixen]. Specifically,
The Cunning Little Vixen is in Líšeň (Brno) dialect. Some of
the vocabulary is unfamiliar to Czechs in Prague, but they
understand most of it, and some Czech schoolchildren study
the original story by Těsnohlídek anyway. For singers, singing in Moravian dialect is no different from singing in Bohemian dialect. The Moravian dialect is actually spoken with
much shorter vowels than in Bohemia, but most Czech singers—Bohemian and Moravian—are careful to distinguish
between short and long vowels whenever the music allows for
it. Janáček went to great lengths to set most long vowels with
longer note values or to create an orchestral texture that
allowed the "bending" of rhythms by the singer (see "Musical
Style" below).

In the case of words like *jsem* [ˈsɛm] (I am), where there
is an initial *j* followed by a consonant, it is common in colloquial speech to leave off the initial *j*, in whatever dialect,
pronouncing the word as [sɛm]. However, even allowing for
the unsophisticated characters in *The Cunning Little Vixen*,
Czech singers follow the highest standards of pronunciation
and sing the initial *j*. Exceptions can be made for vocal con-
siderations and in a few other instances, explained in detail in
Singing in Czech, chapter 2. Any exceptions, however, are
just that—rare exceptions. Otherwise, just sing what is written.
In the case of *jsem*, Janáček simply writes *sem* when he wants
the colloquial version.

Interestingly, the character Lapák, the dog, is the only one
in the whole opera that does not speak in Moravian dialect.
He speaks "standard" Czech instead. Perhaps it is because
Lapák has dedicated himself to art that his speech is more
formal.

Musical Style

Folksong

Janáček's style and influences encompass several main areas, all very apparent in *Příhody lišky Bystroušky*. First is Moravian folk music, which Janáček and his collaborator František Bartoš collected and studied for years. This labor resulted in a large collection of Moravian folksongs published by Bartoš and Janáček in 1892, as well as quite a few wonderful volumes of selected folksongs for which Janáček wrote accompaniments (see Cheek 2001, 217–26).

In his own works, Janáček first fully integrated folk music into his style with the opera *Jenůfa*. In *Příhody lišky Bystroušky*, Těsnohlídek, author of the original novel *Liška Bystrouška* [The vixen Bystrouška] contributed fourteen lines of verse to Janáček's libretto, from which Janáček chose seven and set them in the style of a folksong (in Act II, sc. ii, rehearsal 11, "Bývalo, bývalo" [There was a time, there was a time]). Těsnohlídek had already quoted a folksong in his original novel (Těsnohlídek 1995, 155), and Janáček set this accordingly—with his own folk-like tune—at the opening of Act III, at Harašta's entrance ("Déž sem vandroval" [When I went wandering]). Janáček added a well-known folk text, again to his own music, at Harašta's second entrance (Act III, reh. 23: "Když jsem já šel okolo hája zeleného" [As I went around the grove]). In between, at rehearsal 15, the Lištičky [Fox Cubs] sing "Běží liška k Táboru" [A vixen is running to Tábor] to a variant of a folk text from a collection compiled by the great Czech poet and historian Karel Jaromír Erben (1811–70), this time using the actual folk melody still learned by most Czech schoolchildren (Tyrrell 1992, 285). Other folk-like music abounds in the opera. In 1926 Janáček delivered a speech in London, citing his overriding musical influence: "I have lived in folksong from childhood. . . . If I grow at all, it is only out of folk music, out of human speech" (Zemanová 1989, 60–61).

Speech Melody

Besides folk music, the main source of Janáček's style was "speech melody." Janáček sought to base his operas on the natural inflections of speech, colored by the emotions of the moment. For years he collected "speech melodies," writing down in music practically every utterance he heard, from a woman calling her chickens to the sound of the chickens peeping, even to the final words of his daughter, Olga. (Czech composer Miloš Štědroň [b. 1942] is preparing an edition of all of Janáček's speech melodies.) The opera *Jenůfa* (*Její pastorkyňa*) was the first of Janáček's works to bear fruit from this study; it was an opera written in *prose*, Janáček's preferred libretto. The rhythmic hallmarks of the Czech language—stress on the first syllable, differentiation of long and short vowels—comes to the fore with this approach and must be mastered by non-Czech singers. The inflection goes beyond this, however. For Janáček, speech melody captured not only the sound of the Czech nation, which had become its own country for the first time just a few years before *The Cunning Little Vixen* was written, but it also captured the very heart and soul of the character on the stage. (See "Stress and Length" and "Leoš Janáček" in Cheek 2001, 103–20, 217.)

Rhythm, Phrasing

Speech melody often gives rise to short rhythmic fragments underscored in the orchestra and derived from the speech melody. Quite a few tempo changes occur in the operas, but there is usually an underlying rhythmic figuration that unifies different sections. Janáček termed his use of rhythmic units *sčasovka*, his own word. For conductors they are often the key to understanding Janáček's tempo changes, which can be otherwise difficult to notate and are therefore often misread.

On the other hand, some tempo changes, usually going from fast to slower, call for another hallmark of Janáček's style—sometimes referred to as the "Brno style" of Janáček interpretation—which allows for no feeling of connection. In these cases, the music just stops and starts, without any attempt to round off the ends of phrases.

Janáček often writes orchestral accompaniments that give singers the freedom to "bend" rhythms slightly to accommodate long vowels, and many Czech singers and conductors promote this. Also, any tendency by non-Czech singers to end a phrase on a strong beat must be avoided. The typical Czech phrase begins on a strong beat and ends on a weak one—most of the time the exact opposite of English!

Orchestration

Janáček's orchestration is unique and sometimes problematic—unique in its wonderful timbres, problematic in its practical execution. In its purest form, a certain timbre for Janáček was as inseparable from its particular melody as a speech melody was bound with the emotions of the moment. He found Beethoven's trios and duets disconcerting, because themes were passed from one instrument to another "routinely." In Janáček, themes that are repeated by other instruments have very special significance. Otherwise, merely giving a melody to another instrument "strips it of its timbre." (See Zemanová 1989, 80–83.) Practically speaking, Janáček occasionally asks for the impossible—either an instrument is incapable of playing certain notes or the balance just does not work. The idea behind the unrealizable notation shines through, however, and these few occurrences can be worked out between the conductor and performers.

Eroticism, Nature, and Love

Another characteristic of Janáček's music is eroticism, especially after 1917, when Janáček met Kamila Stösslová (1892–1935). A woman thirty-eight years younger than Janáček, she served as the inspiration for several of his greatest works, beginning with *Zápisník zmizelého* [The diary of one who vanished], and including *Kát'a Kabanová*, *Věc Makropulos*, and the String Quartet no. 2. Janáček developed a friendship with Stösslová that lasted until his death, and hundreds of letters survive from their correspondence. In the score of *The Cunning Little Vixen* that he gave to Stösslová, Janáček made a reference to Act II, sc. iv, reh. 77 (Tyrrell 1994, 168): "In every work of mine there is at least a shadow of your soul. It is in this work when they cry *chcu* [I want (you)]!"

Janáček sought to express the beauty of life and nature, themes that in many ways reach their musical fruition in *Příhody lišky Bystroušky*. This opera celebrates nature and life, and the wonder of their eternal renewal. Like many Czechs, Janáček had a strong connection to nature and was very at home in his garden, the forest, or the countryside. These provided no end of inspiration, joy, and even wisdom. His occupation with *The Cunning Little Vixen* carried over into another work from the same time, 1925, the *Concertino*. A "small musical joke," its four movements for piano and chamber ensemble depict a hedgehog, squirrels, owls, and other creatures (Zemanová 1989, 108–10). One note for singers and coaches—*Příhody lišky Bystroušky* is the most impressionistic of Janáček's operas; he chose this palette the better to depict the world of nature. Many of the singers' entrances can be learned more easily if it is kept in mind that they often begin a whole tone from preceding material.

Finally, the redemptive power of love also recurs throughout Janáček's operas, most notably in *Jenůfa*. In *The Cunning Little Vixen*, too, Janáček writes how the vixen is transformed from a thief and rogue through love (Tyrrell 1992, 295):

> For me it was confirmation that ordinary people don't take evil as a lasting stigma. It happened—and is no more. . . . My Vixen is like that, too: she stole, she throttled [chickens] but besides that she is also capable of noble thoughts. . . . The Vixen falls in love, genuinely in love. . . . Family happiness.

Janáček tended to use the following pitches as a motive expressing love:

This motive occurs, for example, in the last song of *The Diary of One Who Vanished*. In *Kát'a Kabanová* it appears in Act I, rehearsal 19, when Kát'a asks Tichon if he loves her. Then, in reply, the orchestra sets up the motive with A-flat to D-flat, but Tichon distorts it with an F-flat. It is sung in Act II of *The Cunning Little Vixen* by Bystrouška, the Datel [Woodpecker], and the chorus, and it is played by the orchestra just before the curtain falls at the end of the entire opera. Its extensive use throughout is noted in context by the author.

Translations

The English translations of Janáček's libretto serve a two-fold purpose. First, there is a word-for-word translation, important for the performers and stage director, as well as interested listeners, in their understanding of what every word means. (Occasionally, the reflexive *si* or *se* cannot be translated by itself and is just translated with a dash.) Second, there is an idiomatic English translation, often necessary to make sense of the very free Czech word order. Whenever possible, though, this translation follows the word order of the Czech, so that, for example, if the Czech sentence ends with the word *láska* [love], and the English translation works fine also ending with the word *love*, this word order is retained so that both the singer and audience will better understand the original. It is not meant to be "poetic," then, but to rather walk the line between a literal and an idiomatic English translation that reflects the original as much as possible. It is also available from the author as surtitles in an altered format.

Translations of Janáček's Czech stage directions are also given. A few are missing from the orchestral score but present in the piano/vocal score, or vice versa, and these are noted. (None of the German stage directions are translated, as Brod's German version often very much altered the original.)

The characters' names with their translations are listed below. In the body of the libretto usually only the Czech name is given.

Organization

Janáček considered designating scenes with numbers in this opera but abandoned the idea. Instead he gave descriptions of each scene, preferring to highlight the flow of one scene into another. (These descriptions are translated below.) However, to aid in the use of this book, the scenes are named with traditional numbers. Whereas previous writers have sometimes numbered all the scenes in the three acts successively from one to nine, this book renumbers the scenes in each act: Act I, sc. i; Act II, sc. i; etc.

The Opera

Background

The origin of Janáček's *Příhody lišky Bystroušky* [The adventures of the vixen Bystrouška; known as *The Cunning Little Vixen*] lies with the Brno newspaper *Lidové noviny* [People's news], the same source as for Janáček's song cycle *Zápisník zmizelého* [The diary of one who vanished] and his *Říkadla* [Nursery rhymes]. Janáček himself was also a contributor of various feuilletons to the paper.

The Czech painter Stanislav Lolek (1873–1936), who had been an apprentice forester, made some 200 sketches depicting a clever vixen who constantly outwits the local forester. One of the editors of *Lidové noviny*, Dr. Bohumil Markalous, came across these drawings and instructed Rudolf Těsnohlídek (1882–1928), a law reporter and feuilletonist at the paper since 1908, to write a story to accompany the illustrations. The result was Těsnohlídek's most successful work, the short novel *Liška Bystrouška* [The vixen Bystrouška], first published in *Lidové noviny* in fifty-one serial installments between April 7 and June 23, 1920, and then in book form in 1921 (Tyrrell 1992, 283–85).

Janáček began work on *Příhody lišky Bystroušky* in early 1922. The opera was finished that same year, but the composer made extensive revisions in 1923, and a few changes as late as 1925 (Tyrrell 1992, 300–301). Janáček met with Těsnohlídek in 1922, but aside from seven lines of the song "Verunko!" which Těsnohlídek wrote for the libretto (see "Folksong" under "Musical Style," above—Těsnohlídek had originally submitted fourteen lines), Janáček wrote his own libretto (Tyrrell 1992, 285).

Janáček's libretto follows Těsnohlídek's novel very closely throughout Act I and the first half of Act II. For the end of Act II, Janáček cut toward the very end of Těsnohlídek's book, to the marriage of the Fox and the Vixen. The rest of the novel had dealt with a series of clever raids that the Vixen made in the winter at the Forester's abode, and an altercation with Harašta, a poultry dealer, whom the Vixen also managed to outsmart. The very end of the novel corresponds to the opera, with the Forester first at the inn and then in the forest dreaming of the little frog. In Act III of his opera, Janáček introduces the struggle with Harašta but from then on rewrites most of the original. Janáček has Harašta shoot and kill Bystrouška, immediately taking the opera to a different level. The Vixen's death is one of several events that causes the Forester to contemplate old age, life, death, youth, and love, and the entire opera ends with the orchestra proclaiming the love motive. What had been a light-hearted novel by Těsnohlídek[1] became a serious opera that celebrates life, love, nature, and life's constant renewal. All these were fitting themes for Janáček as he approached his seventieth birthday in 1924. The final scene of the opera, "The Forester's Farewell," was performed at the memorial service of Janáček. He died in 1928, the same year as Těsnohlídek.[2]

Janáček's *Příhody lišky Bystroušky* had its premiere in Brno on November 6, 1924, and in Prague on May 18, 1925. For the Prague production, the Czech painter Josef Čapek (1887–1945), brother of famed writer Karel Čapek, was the set and costume designer. In the initial stages of composition Janáček described the opera as "A merry thing with a sad end" (Tyrrell 1994, 37). Before writing a note, he revealed to the *Lidové noviny* in 1921, "It will be an opera as well as a pantomime [mime]." The ballet/mime elements were thus planned from the beginning, and Janáček noted *balet* in his copy of the novel where he wanted these parts to occur (Tyrrell 1992, 287). In the first version of the autograph, Janáček described the opera as a *bajka* [fable]. Later, in a letter the writer and critic Max Brod (1884–1968), he said he would title it as an *opera-idyll*. Finally, he simply called it *opera*, although he later described it as a *forest idyll* in 1927 (Tyrrell 1992, 296, 302).

Max Brod was the friend and biographer of both Kafka and Janáček, and he translated most of Janáček's operas into German. He found Janáček's libretto to *The Cunning Little Vixen* "strange" and sought to "clarify" it in its German version. His greatest change was to elevate Terynka into the love interest of the Pastor, the Schoolmaster, and the Forester, instead of just the Schoolmaster (and later, Harašta), and to make her a parallel to the Vixen. Brod even turns her into a gypsy. In the original novel, Terynka is barely mentioned, and she and her brother are the successful owners of a large candy shop (Těsnohlídek 1995, 74). Janáček expands the references to her in his opera, and she becomes a mysterious figure, because she is never seen. Still, although Janáček allowed some of Brod's alterations in the German translation, he held that human and animal similarities should not be overtly symbolic. He responded to Brod's changes in a letter of 1925: "The source of possible misunderstandings was and is the pairing [of] the Vixen Bystrouška-Terynka" (Tyrrell 1992, 298). This is further explored below, under "Characters."

The Cunning Little Vixen remains first and foremost a celebration of life—with all its adversities, hopes, dreams, disillusionment, joy, and love—and its eternal renewal in nature. Janáček bemoaned the attempt of German critics to seek more symbolism in the work. It is interesting to note, however, that the forest has been a recurrent site of self-discovery and growth throughout history, and is no less true in this opera.

The Vixen is transformed when she finds love there; the Forester gains wisdom there; and even the Schoolmaster and the Pastor reveal there what they hid from the world in the inn—all while the Vixen's eyes glow in the darkness. The humans (with the exception of Harašta) find truths when they are in the forest, and through contact with the Vixen, who of all the characters is most a creature of nature.

As esteemed caretakers of the mind, the soul, and nature, the Schoolmaster, Pastor, and Forester are symbols too, or at least representatives of different parts of society that must all deal with life, love, youth, and old age in their own way. Těsnohlídek writes how Harašta and Bystrouška are cut from the same cloth—they understand one another because they both survive from poultry (Těsnohlídek 1995, 155–56). In him she meets her match, and for Janáček Harašta is the only one who is able to outwit the Vixen. In Janáček's version, he even marries the mysterious Terynka, whom he clothes in the Vixen's fur.

Scene Descriptions

I. Jednání:
Jak chytili Bystroušku.
Bystrouška na dvoře
    jezerské myslivny.
Bystrouška politikem.
Bystrouška zdrhla.

Act I:
How they caught Bystrouška.
Bystrouška at the courtyard of
    "Lake Lodge."
Bystrouška in politics.
Bystrouška gets the hell out.

II. Jednání:
Bystrouška vyvlastňuje.
Bystrouščiny zálety.
Bystrouščiny námluvy
    a láska.

Act II:
Bystrouška dispossesses.
Bystrouška's love affairs.
Bystrouška's courtship
    and love.

III. Jednání:
Bystrouška nadběhla
    Haraštovi z Líšně.
Jak uhynula Liška
    Bystrouška.

Act III:
Bystrouška outran
    Harašta from Líšeň.[3]
How the Vixen Bystrouška died.

Malinká Bystrouška „jak   The baby Bystrouška "the spit-
by mámě z oka vypadla."   ing image of the mother."

Characters

Below are the characters as listed by Janáček, with their
translated names. Some of the cast members are not listed in
the front of the score, or they are named slightly differently
within the score. These are noted in brackets. Also note the
following: Pásek's name could be translated as *little belt* or
little waist, amusing because he probably has quite a paunch.
Lišák, which translates simply as *fox*, is sometimes sung by a
high mezzo. (A few productions have even used a tenor, but
not during Janáček's lifetime.) As for Bystrouška, originally
Těsnohlídek used the name *Bystronožka*, which means *Fast
Feet*. However, the printers made a mistake, and thus the
name *Bystrouška* was born (Simeone 1997, 48). *Bystrouška*
has sometimes been translated to mean *Little Sharp Ears*, but
it more literally means just *Sharpie*.

The name *Chocholka* could be translated as *crested hen*,
since a *chochol* refers to a bird's crest or tuft of feathers.
(Some Czechs refer to a person whose hair stands on end,
maybe soon after getting out of bed, as a *Chocholáč*.) For
what it is worth, the dog Lapák was a dachshund in the
original novel (Těsnohlídek 1995, 87).

Revírník is translated as *Forester*. A *revírník* is a head
myslivec [gamekeeper], each of whom may also be a *lovec*
[hunter]. So, while a *revírník* is also a *myslivec*, not every
myslivec is a *revírník*. A *revírník* was in charge of a *revír*,
which was usually a large part of a forest assigned to his care.
He usually lived in a *myslivna* [gamekeeper's lodge]. Part of
the *revírník*'s duties was to watch for poachers (like Harašta)
and to help keep the animal population balanced. The
revírník's underling was called *hajný* (see this character in
Dvořák's *Rusalka*), who often lived in a house called a
hajenka. The origins of these occupations lie in a former era
when land was owned either by the aristocracy or the Catholic
Church. Today, a *myslivec* refers to a person who has passed a

state gamekeeper's test (*myslivecké zkoušky*), which allows him to carry a rifle and participate in hunts.[4]

Farář has been translated by some as *parson*, by others as *priest*. A *farář* is like a Catholic *pastor*, a priest in charge of a village chapel. He is, then, also roughly equivalent to an Anglican *vicar*. So, similar to the *revírník*, while every pastor is a priest, not every priest is a pastor. The *farář* lived in a *fara*, a vicarage close to a village chapel.

The Pastor, Forester, and Schoolmaster (who is also always a trained musician) represent the village intelligentsia, which is why they hang out together in the inn.

Janáček was very pleased with the original Brno production, but he made the following suggestions: both the choruses of Slípky [Hens] and Lištičky[5] [Fox Cubs] should be cast with children, and the parts of the Kohout, Chocholka, and Lapák should be sung by girls of about fifteen years old. Then, he wrote, their voices would be well differentiated from those of the humans (Tyrrell 1992, 293–94). The voices for these characters had the wrong quality. If the opera is cast with college students, there should be no problem in finding smaller voices and body types. The Lištičky and the Malá Bystrouška are definitely better with children's voices.

The symbols Janáček has used below (*, +, Δ, and ❑) designate characters to be portrayed by the same singer, most of which suggest animal-human parallels. It appears that at the beginning stages of composing the opera, Janáček explored and abandoned many parallels between the humans and the animals. What he ended up with appears below, and it seems to suggest a general portrayal more of man's unity with nature than of specific shared character traits, except, perhaps, in the link between the Badger and the Pastor. Note, especially, the link between the Kohout and the Sojka, an animal-animal parallel! This implies that some of the double roles are merely practical indications to help reduce the size of the unusually large cast, some of which only have a phrase or two to sing, or even only a couple of words. When Max Brod worked with Janáček on the German translation, Brod asked for a stronger connection between the Priest and the Badger, resulting in the addition of the "Milostpán" chorus toward the end of the second scene in Act II, to parallel the chorus of animal creatures also singing "Milostpán" in the first scene of Act I. This is often cut in Czech productions, however, even though Janáček "completely agreed" with Brod's idea (Tyrrell 1992, 300). Other than this, German productions ignore the rest of Janáček's parallels. However, as mentioned previously, Brod also greatly expanded the parallel between the unseen girl Terynka and the Vixen in his German translation, greatly altering the original Czech in the process (Tyrrell 1992, 297–99). Janáček let this stand but was more than content with his original conception. After very critical reviews of the German premiere in Mainz, Janáček wrote in 1927:

> *The Vixen* is a forest idyll; only a hint should
> surface of the sameness of our cycle and that of
> animal life. That is enough—it is true that for most
> this symbolism is too little. (Tyrrell 1992, 302)

Why, then, the mime/ballet in Act I, sc. ii, in which Bystrouška dreams of being a girl? The music is some of the most beautiful in the entire opera. In Act II, sc. iv, the Vixen explains to the Fox: "I have a human upbringing." When the Forester beat her, though, she attacked him and fled to the forest, "And from then on, I'm an animal." So, are we seeing the "human upbringing" in her dream? She cries in the middle of her dream, lamenting her captivity and the forced transition to human life. Perhaps, since her dream occurs in the middle of her captivity, she simply dreams of freedom, which would be hers were she human. Freedom and love—Bystrouška has just said she does not know love, she is alone, and her beautiful "girl music" abounds with intimations of the love motive. Being human could perhaps bring her both the freedom and the love she desires.

Osoby	Characters
Revírník, baryton	Forester, baritone
* Paní revírníková, alt	The Forester's wife, alto
+ Rechtor, tenor	Schoolmaster, tenor

Δ Farář, bas

Harašta, obchodník drůbeží,
bas

Pásek, hostinský, sborový tenor

Bystrouška, soprán

Paní Pásková, chot' hostinského,
sborový soprán

Lišák, soprán

Malá [Malinká] Bystrouška,
dětský soprán

Frantík⎤
        ⎬ klucí,
Pepík ⎦ sborový soprán

Lapák, pes,
mezzo soprán

❑ Kohout, soprán

Chocholka, slípka,
soprán

Cvrček⎤
      ⎮
Kobylka ⎬ dětské hlasy
      ⎮ sopránové
Skokánek⎦

Pastor, bass

Harašta, poultry dealer, bas

Pásek, innkeeper,
chorus tenor

Bystrouška [Sharpie],
soprano

Mrs. Pásek, wife of the
innkeeper,
chorus soprano

Fox, soprano

Little Bystrouška,
child soprano

Frantík⎤
       ⎬ boys,
Pepík ⎦ chorus soprano

Lapák, dog,
mezzo soprano

Rooster, soprano

Chocholka, [crested] hen,
soprano

Cricket⎤
       ⎮
Grasshopper ⎬ soprano
       ⎮ children's
Little frog ⎦ voices

[Balet:]	[Ballet:]
Muška	Little fly
Vážka [Modrá vážka],	Dragonfly [Blue dragonfly],
[Bystrouščin dívčí zjev],	[Bystrouška's human form],
ježek, veverky,	hedgehog, squirrels,
havět' lesní,	forest creatures,
[malinká lištička], balet	[small fox cub], ballet

Datel, alt	Woodpecker, alto
+ Komár, tenor	Mosquito, tenor
Δ Jezevec, bass	Badger, bass
* Sova, alt	Owl, alto
☐Sojka, soprán	Jay, soprano

[Also, choruses:]

Act I:
Slípky, SA   Hens, SA [preferably children]

Act II:
Lesní havět', SA   Forest creatures, SA
Sbor, SA   Chorus, SA [often cut]
Hlas lesa, SAATTBB   Voice of the forest, SAATTBB [offstage

Act III:
Lištičky[5], SA   Fox Cubs, SA [preferably children]

Ranges, Pronunciation of Names

Revírník [rɛviːrɲiːk]   Paní revírníková [paɲiː
Forester   rɛviːrɲiːkovaː] Forester's
                                          wife

Rechtor [rɛxtɔr]
Schoolmaster

Farář [faraːŘ] Pastor

Harašta [ɦaraʃta] (Poultry
dealer)

Pásek [paːsɛk] (Innkeeper)

Bystrouška [bɪstrɔuʃka]
(Vixen)

Paní Pásková [paɲiː
paːskɔvaː]
Mrs. Pásek

Lišák [lɪʃaːk] Fox

Malá Bystrouška
[malaː bɪstrɔuʃka]
Little Bystrouška

Frantík [frantʼiːk] (Boy)

Pepík [pɛpiːk] (Boy)

Lapák [lapaːk] (Dog)

Kohout [kɔfiɔut] Rooster

Chocholka [xɔxɔlka]
Crested hen

Cvrček [t͡svr̥t͡ʃɛk]
Cricket

Kobylka [kɔbɪlka]
Grasshopper

Skokánek [skɔkaːnɛk]
Little frog

Datel [datɛl]
Woodpecker

Komár [kɔmaːr]
Mosquito

Jezevec [jɛzɛvɛt͡s] Badger

Sova [sɔva] Owl

Sojka [sɔⁱka] Jay

Lesní havět' [lɛsɲiː fiavjɛt']
Forest creatures

Sbor [zbɔr] Chorus

Hlas lesa [ɦlas lɛsa]   Muška [muʃka] Little fly
Voice of the forest   Vážka [vaːʃka] Dragonfly
Lištičky [lɪʃt'ɪt͡ʃkɪ] Fox Cubs   Ježek [jɛʒɛk] Hedgehog
Veverky [vɛvɛrkɪ] Squirrels

Synopsis

Act I
Scene i
   The scene opens on a black, dry glen in the afternoon
summer sun. A badger, smoking a long pipe, pokes his head
out of his lair while small flies and a blue dragonfly perform a
ballet. They all leave as the Forester enters, just as exhausted
as the night after his wedding. While he sleeps, a cricket and
grasshopper dance a waltz, and a drunken mosquito tries to
join in the fun. A little frog hops in and chases the mosquito.
The baby vixen Bystrouška [Sharpie] enters and is curious
about how the frog would taste. In a panic, the frog jumps on
the Forester's nose, waking him up. The Forester catches sight
of the baby vixen and takes her away as a pet for his children.
The blue dragonfly looks in vain for Bystrouška.

Scene ii
   It is now autumn, and the afternoon sun shines on the
courtyard of the Forester's lodge. The Forester's wife com-
plains that the Vixen has fleas. Bystrouška moans, and the dog
Lapák chastises her—he has more cause to groan. He has had
a very lonely life, suffering during the months of lovemak-
ing, so that he has had to dedicate himself to art by composing songs. Moreover, the Forester whips him for singing at
night. It is ironic, Lapák says, that he sings without knowing
love. The Vixen replies that she, too, knows nothing of love,
only what she used to hear the starlings gossip about. Lapák
tries to make a pass at Bystrouška, but she knocks him down
and he cowers away into the trash pile.
   The Forester's children, Pepík and Frantík, run into the
courtyard. Pepík grabs Bystrouška, and Frantík torments her
with a stick. Bystrouška bites Pepík's leg and tries to run
away. Hearing Pepík cry, the Forester's wife runs from the
house and calls her husband, who captures the Vixen and ties

her up. She is left all alone as the others go into the house.

It grows dark, and the Vixen cries in her sleep as she dreams of being a girl. Dawn approaches, and the chickens, Lapák, and the Vixen come to life in the courtyard. All berate the Vixen, especially the rooster. Bystrouška calls the hens to a revolution, to bring in a new order in which their lives will not be ruled over by the rooster's lust. When the hens fail to buy this idea, the Vixen says she will bury herself alive rather than face their backwardness. Horrified, the rooster and hens go to see if she is dead. Bystrouška then grabs the rooster and strangles hen after her. Hearing the mayhem, the Forester's wife runs in hysterically and calls her husband. The Forester hits Bystrouška, but she bites through the rope, knocks him down, and escapes into the forest.

Act II
Scene i

It is late afternoon at the lair of the Badger. Bystrouška calls into the lair and the Badger shouts at her to go away. The Vixen calls to the forest creatures to witness how unfair the Badger is toward a poor creature like her. As they side with the Vixen, the Badger strikes her for mocking him and threatens to take her to court. In response, Bystrouška fouls the Badger's lair so that he is forced to abandon it. He takes his pipe, wipes away a tear, and leaves as Bystrouška victoriously slips into her new home.

Scene ii

At Pásek's inn, the Forester and the Schoolmaster are drinking and playing cards in the men's sitting room next to the bar. The Pastor joins them, looking very much like the Badger as he enters with a pipe and speaks of moving to a new home. The Forester teases the Schoolmaster about his present and past loves. The Schoolmaster gets back at him by asking him about the Vixen. The Pastor pontificates in Latin, admonishing men to beware of giving their bodies to women. By now it is early morning, and the Schoolmaster rushes off, apparently to a woman. The innkeeper Pásek warns the Pastor that his new tenants are angrily approaching to confront him. The Pastor, too, rushes off. The tipsy Forester calls for another drink. Pásek teases him about the Vixen's escape, and the Forester teeters off in a huff.

Scene iii

It is night in the forest, and a path is lit by moonlight. A blooming sunflower stands alongside a fence. The drunken Schoolmaster walks up the path, using a stick for support. Bystrouška runs in behind the sunflower, and when it rustles the Schoolmaster imagines he is hearing music. Then, the wind blows the sunflower, and the Schoolmaster thinks he is seeing Terynka, a woman he has loved in vain for twenty-five years. He runs toward the sunflower to embrace it, falls over the fence, and hides as the Pastor enters reciting platitudes. As Bystrouška's eyes shine from the bushes, the Pastor recalls his past love, Susannah, who betrayed him when he was a theology student. Both the Pastor and the Schoolmaster are startled to hear the Forester shouting nearby, in pursuit of Bystrouška. All run for their lives as he starts shooting his rifle at her.

Scene iv

It is a summer moonlit night. Bystrouška is in awe of the handsome Fox, a true gentleman and possibly the first Fox she has laid eyes on since she was a baby. As the Fox listens to her speak about her life he is equally smitten, saying she is the ideal modern woman. When he leaves to go find her a rabbit, the Vixen questions her strange, new feelings and discovers her own beauty. She realizes she has found love. The Fox returns with a rabbit, and their talk becomes more and more intimate. Finally, the Fox passionately embraces Bystrouška, but she is terrified and repulses him. In despair, the Fox declares his love for her and kisses her. The Vixen cries, and the Fox asks if she wants him, too. She answers that she does, and they slip into her lair.

The blue dragonfly flies in and dances a short ballet. Then the Owl flies in with the Jay, and the Owl gossips with her about Bystrouška's shocking behavior with the Fox. As the sun rises, the Vixen comes crying from her lair, followed by the confused Fox. When she whispers to him that she is pregnant, the Fox immediately calls for the pastor—the Woodpecker. The Woodpecker quickly marries them, and all the forest animals join in a jubilant wedding dance.

Act III
Scene i

It is a clear autumn noon day at the edge of a clearing in the forest. The poultry dealer Harašta enters with an empty basket on his back, singing a folksong. The Forester watches him from a distance. Harašta spies a dead hare, but leaves it alone when he sees the Forester approach. Harašta confides to the Forester that he will soon marry none other than Terynka. The Forester is surprised, but then he confronts Harašta about poaching. Harašta denies it and points out the dead hare he found but left well alone. The Forester sees that the hare is surrounded by Bystrouška's footprints, so he sets a trap for her and leaves. Harašta departs in the other direction, and Bystrouška, the Fox, and their Fox Cubs run in, the cubs singing a folksong and dancing. They run to the hare, and the Vixen quickly realizes a trap has been set for them. The Fox flirts with Bystrouška about having more cubs. All except the Vixen hide as Harašta approaches with his basket, now full of chickens. Bystrouška feigns an injury, limping from place to place, while Harašta tries to get a good aim with his rifle. She leads him to uneven ground where he falls and breaks his nose. The Vixen then pounces on the basket of chickens, and feathers fly everywhere. Harašta, however, recovers his rifle, and shoots at the scattering foxes, mortally wounding the Vixen.

Scene ii

The Forester is talking to the Schoolmaster and Mrs. Pásek in the garden at the inn. Pásek is away, and the Pastor has moved to Stráň, where he writes of being homesick. The Forester relates how the Vixen must be dead, since her lair has been abandoned. He tries to tease the Schoolmaster, but the Schoolmaster declares that Terynka is getting married today. Mrs. Pásek says that Terynka has a new muff, which must be from the Vixen. The Forester backs off when he sees that the Schoolmaster has shed a tear. Suddenly the Forester decides to pay for his beer and leave early. He'll go to the forest, and then home. His dog Lapák is too old now to leave home, and the Forester is feeling old, too.

Scene iii

The scene is like the opening of the opera—a black, dry ravine in the sunshine after rain. The Forester walks in, and the mushrooms remind him of his youth, when he and his wife packed mushrooms the day after their wedding. They trampled many of them as they were blinded by love and stole kiss after kiss. The Forester's love of nature reveals itself as he poetically describes the spiritual happiness that comes when the forest and love blossom year after year. He falls asleep smiling, and all the animals appear among the rustling trees. In his dream the Forester rises lamenting the absence of Bystrouška. A tiny vixen, the spitting image of her mother, runs up to him. He tries to catch her but instead grabs hold of a little frog. The Forester is amazed to see the frog again. But no, the little frog explains, that was his grandfather, who used to talk a lot about the Forester. Stunned, the Forester drops his rifle to the ground.

Duration

Act I 25'
Act II 35'
Act III 30'
Total length   1 hr., 30'

Acts I and II are often performed together, with one intermission after Act II.

Act I

I. Jednání
Act I [Scene i]

Černý, suchý žleb.
Black, dry hollow/channel/glen.

Odpolední letní slunce.
Afternoon summer sun.

Opona. Curtain.

V pozadí jeviště doupě jezevcovo.
At the back of the stage the lair of a badger.

Jezevec vystrkuje z doupěte hlavu, kouří z dlouhé dýmky.
The badger sticks out his head from the lair; he smokes from a long pipe.

Mušky krouží okolo (baletní výkon)
Small flies whirl around (ballet performance)

Modrá vážka (baletní výkon)
Blue dragonfly (ballet performance)

Modrá vážka i mušky uletí.
The blue dragonfly and the small flies fly away.

Jezevec zaleze.
The badger goes back in.

Revírník: (s puškou na rameni, uřícen, vzdychne si)
                    (with his rifle on his shoulder, sweating, he sighs)

[dɔstanɛmɛ   bɔːŘku]

Dostaneme [1]**bóřku.**
We're going to have   storm.

We're going to have a storm.

(Utírá si pot s čela.) (He wipes the sweat from his brow.)

[spɔlɛfinu sɪ   na ‿ xvɪltʃɪtʃku]

[2]**Spolehnu si   na   chvilčičku.**
I'll rest   myself for little while.

I'll lie down for a little while.

[paɲiːmaːmɲɛ   řeknu   ʒɛ [i]smɛ tʃɛkalɪ na ‿ pɔbɛrtɪ]

Panímáme   řeknu, že jsme čekali na poberty!
To "old lady"/"missus" I'll say that we waited for thieves!

I'll say to my wife that we were lying in wait for thieves!

Cvrček a kobylka (s malým kolovrátkem)
Cricket and grasshopper (with a small barrel-organ)

Revírník:

[ʔuvjeřiː   fʃak   jɛ   dɔbraːk   ʒɛnskaː]

Uvěří,   však   je   dobrák   ženská.
She'll believe, certainly she is good-natured person female.

She'll believe me; she's certainly a kind-hearted woman.

(usedne si pod keř klokočový.)
(He sits down under a [3]bladder-nut shrub.)

[jak raːnɔ pɔ‿ svatɛbɲiː nɔt͡sɪ jɛ tadɪ]

Jak ráno po [4]svatební noci je tady.
Like morning after wedding night is here.

Here it's like the morning after my wedding night.

[takɛː ⁱsɛm bɪl tak zmatrɔvanɛː]

Také jsem byl tak [5]zmatrované!
Also I was so exhausted!

I was also so exhausted!

Cvrček a kobylka (baletní výkon)
Cricket and grasshopper (ballet performance)

[ʔa tɪ mɔja flɪntɔ kamaraːtkɔ mɔja]

A ty [6]moja flinto, kamarádko moja,
And you my rifle, friend my,

And you, my rifle, my friend,

[pɔjtʼ na‿ mɔjɛ starɛː mɪslɪvɛt͡skɛː sr̩t͡sɛ]

pojď na moje staré [7]myslivecké srdce!
come to my old gamekeeper's heart!

come to my old gamekeeper's heart!

[nɛbr̩blɛʃ   nɛtraːpiːʃ   sɛmka   patŘiːʃ]

Nebrbleš,   **netrápíš,**   **semka**   **patříš.**
You don't grumble,   you don't annoy,   here   you belong.

You don't grumble, you don't pester, you belong here.

(Usíná.) (He falls asleep.)

Cvrček:

[kmɔtŘɛŋka   zakɔnt͡sɛrtɔvala   sɪ   takɛː]

[8]**Kmotřenka,** **zakoncertovala** **si** **také.**
Neighbor,   you would perform   also.

Neighbor, you should make music, too.

Kobylka:

[jɛn : nɛbudɛlɪ   kmɔtŘiːt͡ʃkɔvɪ   vad'ɪt]

Jen   **nebude-li**   **kmotříčkovi**   **vadit,**
Only   it will not-if   to dear neighbor   be a bother,

Only if it won't bother you, dear neighbor,

[ʒɛ   sɪ   pɔtr̩piːm   na ‿ starɔdaːvnɛː   triːlɛ]

že   **si**   **potrpím**   **na**   **starodávné**   **trýle.**
that   I am particular   about   old-time   trills.

that I'm particular about old-time trills.

[9]see note

Tempo valčíku
Waltz tempo

Komár: (podnapilý, baletní výkon) (tipsy, ballet performance)

[sakva   sakva   sakulaⁱda]

Sakva,   sakva,   sakulajda!
Damn,   damn,   whoo-whee!

Damn, damn, whoo-whee!

[10]see note

Skokánek: (chytá komára) (goes after the mosquito)

(Komár uskočí) (The mosquito dodges)
[brrɛkɛtɛ   brrɛkɛtɛ]

Brekete!   Brekete!

Brekete! Brekete!

Komár:

[t͡sɔ   xt͡sɛʃ   klut͡ʃɪskɔ   t͡sɪzɛː]

Co   chceš,   klučisko   cizé?
What   do you want,   rascal   strange/foreign?

What do you want, rascal?

(Utíká) (he runs away)

Skokánek: Komár:

[brrɛkɛtɛ]   [sakva   zavřɪ   ju]

Brekete!   **Sakva,   zavři   ju!**
                        Damn,   close   it!

Brekete!   *Damn, shut up!*

[11]Malinká Bystrouška: (vběhne a zarazí se při pohledu na skokánka.
Skokánek hrůzou ustrne.) (runs in and stops at the sight of the frog.
The·frog, horrified, freezes on the spot.)

Komár:

[gdɛs   bɪl   gdɪʒ   fiřmɲɛlɔ]

Kdes   byl,   [12]když   hřmělo?
Where were you   when   it was thundering?

Where were you when it was thundering?

(Uteče.) (He runs away.)

(Malinká) Bystrouška:
(se zadívá na Skokánka) (fixes her gaze on the frog)

[mamɪ   mamɪ   t͡sɔ jɛ tɔ   t͡sɔ   jɛ   tɔ]

Mami!   Mami!   Co je to? Co   je   to?
Mommy! Mommy! What is that? What is   that?

Mommy! Mommy! What is that? What is that?

[ji: sɛ tɔ   ji: sɛ tɔ]

¹³**Jí** se to? ¹³**Jí** se to?
Eats one that? Eats one that?

Do you eat it? Do you eat it?

(Skokánek zděšeně uskočí a padne Revírníkovi zrovna na nos.)
(The frog, in a panic, jumps away and lands right on the Forester's
nose.)

Revírník: (probudí se) (he wakes up)

[sɛtsakrapɛs   pɔtvɔra   studɛna:]

¹⁴**Setsakrapes!**   **potvora**   **studená!**
Good heavens!   bastard   cold!

Good heavens! Cold bastard!

(Rozhlíží se a spatří malou Bystroušku.)
(He looks around and catches sight of the little Bystrouška.)

(Vynoří svou dravčí tvář z houští a jako šelma polapí Bystroušku.)
(He sticks his wild-looking face out of the thicket, and like a wild
beast he grabs Bystrouška.)

[tɔʃ   tɪ   tak   kujɔ:nɛ]

Tož   **ty**   **tak?**   **Kujóne!**
Then   you   so?   Rascal!

What do we have here? Rascal!

Bystrouška: (úpí) (whimpers)

[mamɪ   mamɪ]

Mami,   mami!
Mommy,   Mommy!

Mommy, Mommy!

Revírník: (vyzdvihne ji jako psa za límec a prohlíží si ji vítězně.)
(he lifts her like a dog by the scruff of the neck and looks her over tri-
umphantly.)

[xa   xa   xa   xa]

Cha,   cha,   cha,   cha!
Ha,   ha,   ha,   ha!

Ha, ha, ha, ha!

Revírník: Bystrouška:

[pɔdr̝iːmɛ si t'ɛ ɦɛskɪ]   [mamɪ   mamɪ]

Podržíme si tě hezky!   **Mami,   mami!**
We'll keep   you nice!   Mommy,   mommy!

We'll hold you tight!   *Mommy, Mommy!*

(Vezme Bystroušku pod paždí, přehodí pušku a odchází.)
(He takes Bystrouška under his arm, slings the rifle over his shoulder,
and leaves.)

Revírník: Bystrouška:

[ʔat' s‿ tɛbɛ majiː d'ɛ͡tska radɔst]   [mamɪ   mamɪ]

ať z tebe mají děcka radost!   Mami,   mami!
let from you have kids pleasure!   Mommy, Mommy!

let the kids have fun with you!   *Mommy, Mommy!*

[Orchestral score here has:
odchází s M. Bystr.   he leaves with the small Bystrouška.]

Revírník: (z dálky) (from far away)

[xa   xa   xa   xa]

Cha, cha, cha, cha.
Ha,   ha,   ha,   ha.

Ha, ha, ha, ha.

Modrá vážka (přiletí a hledá marně Bystroušku)
Blue dragonfly (flies in and looks in vain for Bystrouška)

[15]see note

(Modrá vážka usedne a složí křídla.)
(The blue dragonfly settles down and folds its wings.)

Proměna   Scene change [Act I, scene ii]

Na dvoře jezerské myslivny. At the courtyard of [16]"Lake Lodge."
Odpolední slunce. Afternoon sun.   Podzim. Autumn.

[17]see note

Opona Curtain

Na pravo z předsíně vystoupí Revírník.
At the right, from the vestibule the Forester appears.

Revírník:

[tɔ   t͡ʃut͡ʃiːʃ   lapaːku]

To   čučíš   Lapáku!?
That   you gawk at   Lapák!?

What are you gawking at, Lapák!?

Paní revírníková: (stojí na prahu) (she stands on the door step)

[dɔnɛsls   jɛn   s ‿ t'iːm   blɛxɪ]

Donesl's   jen   s   tím   blechy!
Brought you   just   with that   fleas!

You just brought fleas with that!

(nalévá do misky mléka.) (she pours milk into a bowl.)
[jɛnɔm   blɛxɪ]

Jenom   blechy!
Only   fleas!

Only fleas!

(Rev. zajde do myslivny.) (The Forester goes into the lodge.)

(Bystr. mlsá a kňučí.)
(Bystrouška laps up [the milk] satisfyingly and whines.)

Bystrouška:

[ʔɔːu ʔɔːu ʔɔːu ʔɔːu]

[18]**Ou,   Ou! Ou, Ou!**

Oh, oh! Oh, oh!

Lapák:		Bystrouška:
[nɛnaři:kɛⁱ tɔlɪk]		[ʔɔːu ʔɔːu]
Nenaříkej tolik!		**Ou, Ou!**
Don't groan so much!		
Don't groan so much!		*Oh, oh!*

Lapák:

[t͡sɔʃ   muːⁱ   ʔɔsamɲeliː   ʒivɔt]

Což   můj   [19]osamělý   život?
What about   my   lonely   life?

What about my lonely life?

[t͡sɔʃ   triːzeɲ   mɛːɦɔ sr̥t͡sɛ   v‿mɲɛsiːt͡siːx laːskɪ]

Což   trýzeň   mého srdce   v měsících lásky,
What about torments of my heart   in months   of love,

What about the torments of my heart in the months of love,

[20]see note

[f‿ʔuːnɔru březnu   ʔɔu]

v únoru, březnu? [21]**Ou!**
in February, March?

in February, March?   Oh!

[ʔɔdːdal ⁱsɛm sɛ   ʔumɲɛɲiː]

[22]**Oddal jsem se   umění.**
I have given myself to   art.

I have given myself to art.

(Bystrouška dívá se na Lapáka na časem dojatě, časem lhostejně.)
(Bystrouška looks at Lapák at times with affection, at times with indifference.)

[vetʃer spiːvaːm smutnɛ piːsɲe saːm sɪ je sklaːdaːm]

Večer zpívám smutné písně, sám si je skládám.
Evening I sing   sad   songs, by myself them I compose.

In the evening I sing sad songs, I compose them myself.

[ʔalɛ za‿tɔ   mnɛ   dʼɛdɛk   spraːskaː ʔɔu]

Ale za to   mne   dědek   spráská. Ou!
But for that me   old man whips.   Oh!

But the old man whips me for it. Oh!

[spiːvaːm ʔa pR̝ɛt͡sɛ nɛviːm t͡sɔ jɛ laːska]

Zpívám **a** **přece** **nevím,** **co** **je** **láska?**
I sing and yet I don't know what is love?

I sing and yet I don't know what love is?

Bystrouška:

[jaː takɪ nɛmaːm skuʃɛnɔstʼɪ v ‿ mɪlɔvaːɲiː]

Já **taky** **nemám** **zkušenosti** **v** **milování.**
I also don't have experience in love making.

I also don't have experience in love making.

[ʔalɛ lɛdat͡sɔs ⁱsɛm vɪslexla ʔɔt ‿ ʃpat͡ʃkuː]

Ale **ledacos** **jsem vyslechla** **od** **špačků,**
But various things I have overheard from starlings,

But I've overheard various things from the starlings,

[ktɛ̝r̝iː ɦɲiːzdʼɪlɪ nad ‿ naʃiːm dɔupjɛtɛm]

kteří **hnízdili** **nad** **naším** **doupětem.**
who nested above our den.

who nested above our den.

[t͡sɔ xviːla dɔxaːzɛlɔ u‿ɲɪx g‿ ɦaːtkaːm prat͡ʃkaːm]

Co chvíla docházelo u nich k hádkám, pračkám.
Very often it came at us to quarrels, fights.

Very often they quarreled and fought.

[vɪt͡ʃiːtalɪ sɪ]

Vyčítali si
They reproached one another

They reproached each other

[ɦrɔznɛː vjet͡sɪ nɛmravnɛː ʔa nɛsluʃnɛː]

hrozné věci nemravné a neslušné,
horrible things immoral and indecent,

with horrible immoral and indecent things,

[ʒɛ stariː ʃpat͡ʃɛk nɛstɪdatiː zaːlɛtɲiːk]

že starý špaček, nestydatý záletník,
that old starling, shameless philanderer,

saying that the old starling, a shameless philanderer,

[prɔvaːdʼiː nɛpR̝iːstɔⁱnɔstʼɪ f ‿ kɔruɲɛ bukuː]

provádí nepřístojnosti v koruně ²³buků.
carries on improper behavior in crown of beeches.

was behaving improperly in the tops of beech trees.

[ʔa   jɛdnɔu   f ‿ sɔbɔtu   pɔ ‿ viːplatʼɛ]

A   jednou,   v   sobotu   po   výplatě,
And   once,   on   Saturday   after   payday,

And once, on the Saturday after payday,

[zakrɔt͡ʃɪl   kr̩kavɛt͡s   s‿ʔɔstr̝iːʒɛm   ʔa   zlɛ   jɛ   spɔr̝aːdal]

zakročil   krkavec   s   ostřížem   a   zle   je   spořádal.
stepped in   raven   with   falcon   and   badly them   beat up.

the raven and the hawk stepped in and beat them up badly.

[ʔɔstatɲɛ   mladʼiː   ʃpat͡ʃtsɪ   nɛbɪlɪ   lɛpʃiː   stariːx]

Ostatně,   mladí   špačci   nebyli   lepší   starých.
For that matter,   young   starlings   weren't   better   of old ones.

*For that matter, the young starlings weren't any better than
the old ones.*

[jɛdɛn   mɲɛl   fir̝iːʃniː   pɔmɲɛr   s ‿ kukat͡ʃkɔu]

Jeden   měl   hříšný   poměr   s   kukačkou.
One   had   sinful   relationship   with   cuckoo.

One had a sinful relationship with a cuckoo.

[naʔut͡ʃil   sɛ   zanaːʃɛt   dɔ ‿ t͡sɪziːɦɔ   fɲiːzda]

Naučil   se   zanášet   do   cizího   hnízda.
He learned   to fill up   to   strange   nest.

He learned to lay eggs in another bird's nest.

[jɪniː   bɪl   nut͡sɛn   plat'ɪt   strat͡sɛ]

Jiný   **byl**   **nucen**   **platit**   **strace**
Another   was   compelled   to pay   to magpie

Another had to pay the magpie

[pɔ‿kɔpet͡ʃku   ʔɔřɛxuː   liːskɔviːx]

po   **kopečku**   [24]**ořechů**   **lískových.**
by   heap   of nuts   of hazel.

alimony in hazelnuts.

[ʔa   t͡sɛra   ʃpat͡ʃkɔva   nɛpɔfilɛdnaː   ʔuʃubranaː]

A   **dcera**   **špačkova**   **nepohledná,**   **ušubraná,**
And   daughter   starling's   ugly,   dirty,

And the starling's daughter, ugly, dirty,

[mɲɛla   znaːmɔst   s‿mladiːm   ɦavranɛm]

měla   **známost**   **s**   **mladým**   **havranem.**
had   acquaintance   with   young   crow.

had an acquaintance with a young crow.

(Lapák chytne Bystroušku za prut. Slípky se rozprchnou.)
(Lapák catches Bystrouška by the tail. The hens scatter.)

(Bystr. povalí Lapáka.) (Bystrouška knocks down Lapák.)

[nɛstɪdɔ   psiː]

Nestydo   psí!
Shameless   dog!

Shameless dog!

(Lapák zaleze na smetiště. Bystr. se přikrčí.)
(Lapák cowers away in the trash pile. Bystrouška crouches down.)

Pepík a Frantík: (vběhnou na dvůr) (they run into the courtyard)
(Pepík chytne Bystroušku a zvedne ji.)
(Pepík catches Bystrouška and picks her up.)

Pepík: (Frantík strká Bystr. proutek pod nos.)
                                  (Frantík pushes a stick under Bystrouška's nose.)
[ʒɛ   nɛviːʃ   t͡sɔ   maːmɛ   maːmɛ   lɪʃku]

Že   nevíš,   co   máme?   Máme   lišku.
That   you don't know   what   we have?   We have   vixen.

I bet you don't know what we have. We have a vixen.

Frantík:

[kɔːʃɛ]

Kóše?   (lehtá Bystr. pod nosem.)
Does she bite?   (he tickles Bystrouška under the nose.)

Does she bite?

Bystrouška: (zlostně) (angrily)

[t͡sɔ pak ⁱsɛm jaː t͡sɔ pak ⁱsɛm jaː ɲaːkɛː pɛs jak lapaːk]

Co   pak jsem já—co pak jsem já ²⁵ňáké pes, jak Lapák?!
What then am I   what then am I   some dog, like Lapák?!

*What do you take me for—what do you take me for, some dog,
like Lapák?!*

Frantík: Bystrouška:

[slɪʃiːʃ   jak   vr̩t͡ʃiː]   [klut͡ʃɪskɔ   ʔuʃmɔːranɛː]

Slyšíš,   jak   vrčí?   Klučisko   ušmórané!
Do you hear how   she growls?   Rascal   dirty!

Do you hear how she growls?   *Dirty rascal!*

Frantík: Bystrouška:

[tɛt' ʔɔbjɛma   ʃt͡ʃagɛlkamɪ] [pR̝ɛstaɲ pR̝ɛstaɲ jɛn ɦɲɪ]

Teď oběma   ²⁶ščagelkami! Přestaň! Přestaň! Jen hni!
Now with both   sticks!   Stop!   Stop!   Just move!

Now with both sticks!   *Stop! Stop!   Just try it!*

Frantík: (čibne ji po nose.) (he strikes her on the nose.)

[ft͡ʃɪl   na ‿ ɲu]

Včil   na   ňu!
Now   on   her!

Now, get her!

Bystrouška:

[ʔudɛrɪls   pɔtɛt͡ʃɛ   kriːf]

²⁷Uderil's,   poteče   krív!
You struck,   it will flow   blood!

You struck me, blood will flow!

(Vrhne se na Pepíka.) (She pounces on Pepík.)

Pepík:

[buː   buː   ʔɔna   mɲɛ   ʔuʒrala   liːtkɔ]

Bú!   Bú!   Ona   mně   užrala   lýtko.
Boo-hoo! Boo-hoo! She   to me   bit   calf.

Boo hoo! Boo hoo! She bit my calf.

(Bystr. ubíhá k lesu, Frantík za ní.)
(Bystrouška runs away toward the forest, Frantík after her.)

[ʔɔna   mɲɛ   sɛʒɛrɛ]

Ona   ²⁸mně   sežere!
She   me   eat up!

She'll eat me up!

Bystrouška: (Bystr. klopýtne.) (Bystrouška stumbles.)

[zdr̩ɦɛː]

Zdrhé!
Get the hell out of here!

Get the hell out of here!

Frantík: Pepík:

[xɪt'tɛ   ju   ʔuʃ   jɪ   maːm]   [buː   buː]]

Chyťte ju!   Už   ji   mám!   **Bú,   bú!**
Catch   her! Already her   I have!   Boo hoo, boo hoo!

Catch her! I've got her already!   *Boo hoo, boo hoo!*

Paní revírníková: Pepík:
(Vyběhne z domu.) (She runs from the house.)

[tɪ   taːtɔ]   [buː]

Ty   táto!   **Bú!**
Hey   dad!   Boo hoo!

Hey, dad!   *Boo hoo!*

Paní revírníková: Pepík:

[jaː   t'ɪ   tu   lɪʃku   vɪkɔpu]   [buː]

Já   ti   tu   lišku   vykopu!   **bú!**
I   to you that vixen   will kick out!

I'll get rid of your vixen!   *Boo hoo!*

[smr̩d'iː tɔ ʔa   zavaziː   ʔa t͡sɔ   ʃkɔdɪ   nad'ɛlaː]

smrdí to a [29]zavazí   a   co   škody   nadělá!
stinks   it and gets in way and what damages causes a lot of!

it stinks and gets in the way and tears up everything!

Pepík: (Revírník napohlavčí Pepíkovi.) (Revírník boxes Pepík's ears.)

[buː]

bú?

         (Pepík prohlíži si kalhoty.) (Pepík inspects his pants.)
Boo hoo?

Revírník: Bystrouška:

[tɔʃ   ju ʔuvaːʒɛmɛ]   [ʔɔu ʔɔu]

Tož [30]**ju uvážeme!**   [31]**Ou, Ou?**
Then   her we'll tie up!   Ouch, ouch?

Let's tie her up, then!   *Ouch, ouch?*

(Uvazuje Bystroušku.) (He ties up Bystrouška.)

(Revírník s pí. rev. zajdou [a [32]Pepíkem] do stavení. Frantík se vytratí,
Lapák zaleze do předsíně. Dvorek se vyprázdní.)
(The Forester and the Forester's wife [and [32]Pepík] go into the house.
Frantík slips away, Lapák creeps away into the vestibule. The courtyard
empties.)

Setmí se. It grows dark.

Bystrouščin dívčí zjev. Bystrouška's girl's figure.
[Bystrouška appears as a girl.] [33]see note

(Bystrouška pláče ze spánku.) (Bystrouška cries in her sleep.)

Bystrouška:

[ʔa ʔa]

a   a!

Ah, ah!

Svítání Dawn
Bystrouščin liščí zjev. Bystrouška's vixen figure.
(Lapák se protahuje.) (Lapák stretches.)

Lapák: (k Bystroušce) (toward Bystrouška)

[mɲɛlas   d'ɛlat   pɔdlɪvaː   mɲɛ]

Mělas   **dělat**   **podlivá**   **mně!**
You should have   done   according to me!

You should have done what I did!

[mɲɛlas   neut'iːkat]   (Kohout se naparuje.)
                                                 (The rooster puts on airs.)

Mělas   **neutíkat!**
You shouldn't have run away!

You shouldn't have run away!

[nɛvɪlɪzɔvat   miːsɛ]

Nevylizovat   **míse!**
Not lick   bowls!

You shouldn't have licked the bowls!

Kohout:

[d'iːveːtɛ sɛ   jak   jɛ   t͡ʃlɔvjɛk   spravɛdlɪveː]

Dívéte   se,   **jak   je**   **člověk**   **spravedlivé!**
  You look   how   is   man   just/fair.

Look how just man is!

(Pí. rev. sype drůbeži.) (Paní revírníková scatters [food] for the poultry.)

[ɦɔɲɪla   naːs   slɛt͡ʃna   lɪʃka]

Honila   nás   slečna   liška,
She hunted   us   Miss   vixen,

Miss Vixen hunted us,

[ʔa   ft͡ʃɪl   nɛviː   kudɪ   kam]

a   včil   neví   kudy   kam?
and   now   she doesn't know   what to do?

and now she doesn't know what to do?

[tɔ   prɔtɔ   ʒɛ   nɛsnaːʃiː   vajiːt͡ʃka]

To   proto,   že   nesnáší   vajíčka,
It   is why that   she doesn't lay   eggs,

It's because she doesn't lay eggs,

[ʒɛ   vɛ ‿ ɦɲiːzd'ɛ   nɛsɛdaː]

že   ve   hnízdě   nesedá!
that   in   nests   she doesn't sit!

she doesn't sit in nests!

[snaːʃɛːtɛ   prat͡suⁱtɛ   ʔa   jaː   vaːm   pɔmɔʒu]

Snášéte,   pracujte,   a   já   vám   pomožu!
Lay,   work,   and   I   you   will help!

Lay, work, and I'll help you!

Slípky:

[mɪ   praˆt͡sujɛm   sna:ʃiːmɛ   mɪ   praˆt͡sujɛm   sna:ʃiːmɛ]

My   pracujem,   snášíme.   My   pracujem,   snášíme.
We   work,   we lay.   We   work,   we lay.

We work, we lay. We work, we lay.

Chocholka: Slípky:

[tr̩p   tr̩p]   [mɪ   praˆt͡sujɛm   sna:ʃiːmɛ]

[34]**Trrrp!   Trrrp!**   **My   pracujem,   snášíme.**
Suffer!   Suffer!   We   work,   we lay.

Suffer! Suffer!   *We work, we lay.*

Chocholka:

[tr̩p   tr̩p   fʃak   zaslɔuʒiːʃ]

Trrrp!   Trp,   však   zasloužíš!
Suffer!   Suffer, surely   you deserve!

Suffer! Suffer, surely you deserve it!

Slípky:

[mɪ   praˆt͡sujɛm   sna:ʃiːmɛ   mɪ   praˆt͡sujɛm   sna:ʃiːmɛ]

My   pracujem,   snášíme.   My   pracujem,   snášíme.
We   work,   we lay.   We   work,   we lay.

We work, we lay. We work, we lay.

Chocholka:

[tr̩p   tr̩p]

Trrrp!   Trrrp!
Suffer!   Suffer!

Suffer! Suffer!

Kohout:

[jɛn   snaːʃeːtɛ   jaː   pɔmɔʒu]

Jen   snášéte,   já   pomožu!
Just   lay,   I   will help!

Just lay, I'll help!

Bystrouška: (vymrští se) (she springs up)

[ɦlɛtʼtɛ   sɛstrɪ   jakeːɦo   maːtɛ   vuːt͡tsɛ]

Hled ˇte,   sestry,   jakého   máte   vůdce!
Observe,   sisters,   what kind   you have   leader!

Observe, sisters, what kind of leader you've got!

[xt͡sɛ   vaːs   prɔ‿   svɔjɛ   xɔutkɪ]

Chce   vás   pro   svoje   choutky,
He wants   you   for   his   lusts,

He wants you for his lust,

[za‿ tɔ bɛrɛ   ʒɔlt   ʔɔt‿ t͡ʃlɔvjɛka]

za   to   bere   žold   od   člověka.
for   it   he takes   pay   from   man.

for that he's paid by man.

(lísavě) (f̦awning)

[druʒɪt͡ʃkɪ   sɛstŘɪt͡ʃkɪ   ʔɔtstraɲtɛ   starɛː   řaːdɪ]

Družičky!   Sestřičky!   Odstraňte   staré   řády!
Friends!   Dear sisters!   Do away with   old   orders!

Friends! Dear sisters! Do away with the old order!

[stvɔřtɛ   nɔviː   svjɛt]

Stvořte   nový   svět,
Create   new   world,

Create a new world

[gdɛ budɛtɛ   rɔvniːm   d'iːlɛm zd'iːlɛt radɔst'ɪ ʔa ʃt'ɛst'iː]

kde   budete   rovným   dílem   sdílet   radosti a   štěstí.
where   you will   with equal   part   share   pleasure and joy.

where you will share equally pleasure and happiness.

Slípky: (chechtají se) (they howl with laughter)

[bɛs ‿ kɔfiɔːta   bɛs ‿ kɔfiɔːta]

Bez   kohóta?   Bez   kohóta?
Without   rooster?   Without   rooster?

Without a rooster? Without a rooster?

Bystrouška:

[natʃ   vaːm   tŘɛba   kɔfiɔuta]

Nač   vám   třeba   [35]kohouta?
For what   for you   is necessary   rooster?

What do you need a rooster for?

[nɛⁱlɛpʃiː   zr̩ŋkɔ   sɛzɔbɛ   saːm]

Nejlepší   zrnko   sezobe   sám,
Best   grain   pecks at   by himself,

He pecks at the best grain himself,

[ʔa   dɔ ‿tʃɛfiɔ   sɛ   mu   nɛxt͡sɛ]

a   do   čeho   se   mu   nechce,
and   to   what   himself   to him   he doesn't want,

and what he doesn't want to do,

[na‿tɔ   sɪ   vaːz ː zavɔlaː]

na to si vás   zavolá.
for it -   you   he calls.

he calls you to do.

Kohout: (rozhorlí se) (he becomes enraged)

[tlama   ɦladɔvaː   slɪbujɛ   ʔɔtstraɲɪt   t͡ʃlɔvjɛka]

Tlama   hladová!   Slibuje   odstranit   člověka,
Muzzle   hungry!   She promises to get rid of man,

Hungry muzzle! She promises to get rid of man,

[ʔabɪ   naːs ː sama   sɛʒrala]

aby   nás   sama   sežrala.
so that   us   by herself she would eat up.

so she could eat us up herself.

Slípky:
            (rozptylují se po dvoře) (they scatter all over the courtyard)
      [vɪda   vɪda   vɪda   vɪda   vɪda]

     Vida!   Vida!   Vida!   Vida!   Vida!
[36]You see! You see! You see! You see! You see!

You see! You see! You see! You see! You see!

Bystrouška:

[nɛʒ   bɪx   jaː sɛ d'iːvala na‿vaʃɪ   zaʔɔstalost]

[37]**Než   bych já se dívala   na vaši   zaostalost,**
Rather than would I   look   at your   backwardness,

Rather than look at your backwardness,

(Vyohrabuje si na smetišti jámu.) (She digs a hole in the trash heap.)

[tɔ   sɛ   rad'ɛⁱ   za‿ʒɪva   pɔfifbiːm]

to   se   raděj   za   živa pohřbím!
it   myself prefer in   alive I will bury!

I prefer to bury myself alive!

(Zahrabuje se.) (She buries herself.)

Chocholka:
                                (s hrůzou) (with horror)

[zbabjɛlt͡ʃɛ   pɔd'iːvɛː sɛ   jɛ lɪ   ʔuʃ   mr̩tvaː]

Zbabělče,   podívé   se,   je-li   už   mrtvá?
Coward,   look,   she is-if already dead?

Coward, see if she's already dead?

(Slípky se zvědavě sbíhají.) (With curiosity, the little hens come to-gether.)

(Bystr. náhle schvátí kohouta a dáví slípku za slípkou.)
(Bystrouška suddenly grabs the rooster and strangles hen after hen.)

(Chocholka běhá jak pomatená.) (Chocholka runs around like a maniac.)

[kɔkɔkɔdaːk   kɔkɔkɔdaːk]

Kokokodák!   **Kokokodák!**
Cock-cock-a-doo!   Cock-cock-a-doo!

Cock-cock-a-doo! Cock-cock-a-doo!

(Pí. revírníková vyběhne zděšena.)
(The Forester's wife runs out alarmed.)

[kɔkɔ   kɔkɔ   kɔkɔ   kɔkɔ]

Koko, koko, koko, koko,
Cock-a, cock-a, cock-a, cock-a,

Cock-a, cock-a, cock-a, cock-a

Paní revírníková: (div nepadne do mdlob) (it's a wonder she does not fall in a faint)

[ʔɔːu]

[38]**Ou?**
Oh?

Oh?

Chocholka:

[kɔkɔkɔdaːk]

Kokokodák!
Cock-cock-a-doo!

Cock-cock-a-doo!

Paní revírníková: Bystrouška:

[ʔɔːu ʔɔu   ʔɔː bɛstɪjɔ]   [xa   xa   xa   xa]

[39]**Ou?   Ou?   Ó, bestio!**   **Cha, cha, cha, cha!**
Oh?   Oh?   Oh, bitch!   **Ha,   ha,   ha,   ha!**

Oh? Oh?   Oh, you bitch!   *Ha, ha, ha, ha!*

Paní revírníková: Bystrouška:

[ʔɔː bɛstɪjɔ]   [xa   xa   xa   xa]

Ó,   bestio!   **Cha, cha, cha, cha!**
Oh,   bitch!   **Ha,   ha,   ha,   ha!**

Oh, you bitch!   *Ha, ha, ha, ha!*

Chocholka:

[kɔkɔdaːk   kɔkɔdaːk   kɔkɔdaːk]

Kokodák,   kokodák,   kokodák!
Cock-a-doo,   cock-a-doo,   cock-a-doo!

Cock-a-doo, cock-a-doo, cock-a-doo!

Paní revírníková :   Chocholka:

[tɪ   slɔtɔ   jɛdna]   [gdɛ   jɛɦɔ   ɲɛʒnɔstˈɪ]

Ty   sloto   jedna!   **Kde   jeho   něžnosti!**
You scoundrel   one!   Where   his   tenderness!

You're nothing but a scoundrel!   *Where is his tenderness!*

Paní revírníková:

[tɔ   maːm   za ‿ tɔ]

To   mám   za   to,
This   I have   for   it,

This is what I get

[ʒɛ   ⁱsɛm   svɛːɦɔ   starɛːɦɔ   blaːzna   ʔupɔslɛxla]

že   jsem   svého   starého   blázna   uposlechla!
that   I have   my   old   fool   listened to!

for listening to my old fool!

Chocholka:

[s ‿   t͡ʃistiːx   vajiːt͡ʃɛk   kuřaːtka   nɛvɪsɛd'iːm]

Z   čistých   vajíček   kuřátka   nevysedím.
From   clear   eggs   chicks   I will not hatch.

From   clear eggs I won't hatch any chicks.

Paní revírníková:

[mɔɦl̩   biːt   s ‿ tɛbɛ   ʃtut͡s]

Mohl   být   z   tebe   štuc.
It could   be   from   you   muff.

You could have been a muff.

(Bystrouška vyskočí, rozhodne se utéci.)
(Bystrouška jumps up, she decides to run away.)

[pɔt͡ʃkeⁱ   pɔt͡ʃkeⁱ   ʔɔː   bɛstɪjɔ]

Počkej,   počkej!   Ó,   bestio!
Wait,   wait!   Oh,   you bitch!

Wait, wait! Oh, you bitch!

Bystrouška: Paní revírníková:

[tɛt'   nɛbɔ   ɲɪgdɪ]   [jɛstlɪ   t'ɛ   nɛvɪkɔpu   ʔɔː   bɛstɪjɔ]

Teď   nebo   nikdy!   Jestli   tě   nevykopu!   Ó, bestio!
Now   or   never!   If   you I don't kick out! Oh, bitch!

Now or never!   *If I don't kick you out! Oh, you bitch!*

Paní revírníková:

[starɛː   zastŘɛl   ju]

⁴⁰Staré,   zastřel   ju!
Old man,   shoot   her!

Old man, shoot her!

⁴¹see note

(Bystr. trhá se na provaze.) (Bystrouška jerks at the rope.)

(Revírník vyjde s obuškem a mlátí Bystroušku.)
(The forester appears with a club and hits Bystrouška.)

Bystrouška:

[nɛbɔjiːm sɛ   t'ɛ gdɪbɪs   bɪl   stɔkraːt   tɔlkɛː]

Nebojím se   tě, kdybys byl   stokrát   tolké!
I am not afraid of you, if you   were   hundred times   big!

I'm not afraid of you, even if you were a hundred times bigger!

Revírník:

[jaː t'ɛ   ʔudɛřiːm na ‿ ɦlavu]

Já   tě   udeřím   na   hlavu.
I   you   will hit on   head.

I'll hit you on the head.

[42]see note

(Bystr. překousne provaz a ubíhá do lesa.)
(Bystrouška bites off the rope and runs away into the forest.)

Bystrouška:

[nɛbɔ jaː   tɛbɛ]

Nebo já   tebe!
Or   I   you!

Or I'll hit yours!

[43]see note

(Povalí a přemetne revírníka, ubíhá.)
(She knocks down the Forester, leaps over him, and runs away.)

Opona   Curtain

Konec I. jednání.   **End of the first act.**

Bystrouška with Lišák, one of the drawings by Stanislav Lolek (1873-1936)
used in the original novel *Liška Bystrouška* (Těsnohlídek 1995, 188). Reprinted
with the permission of Ctibor Lolek.

Act II

II. Jednání.
Act II [Scene i]

Opona Curtain

Les, doupě jezevcovo. The forest, the lair of the Badger.
Pozdní odpoledne. Late afternoon.

Bystrouška:
(dívá se jezevci do doupěte) (she looks into the Badger's lair)

[ʔax]

Ach!
Ah!

Ah!

Jezevec:

[gdɔ   pak   tɔ   tu   vřɛːskaː]

Kdo   pak   to   tu   vřéská?
Who   then   it   here   screams?

Who is screaming here?

Bystrouška:

[ja: ja: mɪlɔstpanɛ]

Já, já, milostpane!
I,   I,   Sir!

I, I, Sir!

(Nakukuje do brlohu způsobně.)
(She peeps into the den in a well-mannered way.)

Jezevec: (rozkřikne se) (he shouts)

[tɪ   slɔtɔ   ʒɛbra:t͡ska: blɛxata:]

Ty   sloto   žebrácká,   ¹blechatá!
You   scoundrel   beggarly,   flea-ridden!

You beggarly, flea-ridden scoundrel!

[ja: t'ɪ   pɔvi:m   pR̝ɛstanɛʃ   t͡ʃut͡ʃet]

Já   ti   povím!   Přestaneš   čučet!
I   to you   say!   Stop   gawking!

I'm telling you! Stop gawking!

Bystrouška:

[xɛ xɛ xɛ xɛ   xɛ xɛ xɛ xɛ]

Che, che, che, che! ²Che, che, che, che!

Ha, ha, ha, ha! Ha, ha, ha, ha!

[pɔvɪdɛː sɪ   bɛstak   maːʃ   jazɪk   liːnɛː]

Povidé   si,   beztak   máš   jazyk   líné!
Chatter,   anyway   [3]you have   tongue   lazy!

Chatter away, anyway you have a lazy tongue!

Lesní havět':

[z ⌣ řɛt͡ʃɔː   sɛ pɔt'iːʃ]

S   řečó   se potíš!
With   talk   you perspire.

[4]*You sweat as you speak!*

Bystrouška:

[pɔd'iːvɛːtɛ sɛ   vaːliː sɛ   tu   jak   mɪlɔstpaːn]

Podívéte   se,   válí   se   tu   jak   milostpán!
Look,   he lounges around   here   like   lord!

[5]*Look, he lounges around here like a lord!*

Lesní havět':

[jak   mɪlɔstpaːn   mɪlɔstpaːn]

Jak   milostpán!   Milostpán!
Like   lord!   Lord!

Like a lord! A lord!

Bystrouška:

[duːm ː maː   ʒɛ   bɪ   sɛ   tam   vɛʃlɪ   tR̬ɪ]

Dům	**má,**	**že**	**by**	**se**	**tam**	**vešli**	**tři**
House	he has	that	would	-	there	fit	three

He has a house that could fit three,

[ʔa xudaːkɔvɪ   vɪnadaː   ʒɛ   sɛ   xt͡sɛ   jɛn   pɔd'iːvat]

a	**chudákovi**	**vynadá,**	**že**	**se**	**chce**	**jen**	**podívat.**
and	to poor one he	bad-mouths	that	-	wants	only	to look.

and he bawls out a poor creature who only wants to have a look.

Lesní havět':   Bystrouška:

[mɪlɔstpaːn]   [lɛʒiː   jak   kraːva   v‿ lɔːt͡sɛ]

Milostpán!	**Leží**	**jak**	**kráva**	**v**	**lóce.**
Lord!	He lies	like	cow	in	meadow.

A lord!   *He lies like a cow in the meadow.*

Lesní havět':

[mɪlɔstpaːn   mɪlɔstpaːn]

Milostpán!	**Milostpán!**
Lord!	Lord!

A lord! A lord!

Jezevec:
(přetáhne Bystroušku) (he hits Bystrouška)
[jaː t'ɪ   daːm   xlaːmat'   tutɛː   pR̩ɛd ‿ naʃɪma]

Já ti   dám   ⁶chlámať̆   tuté   před   našima,
I   to you give   mocking   here   in front of our,

I'll teach you a lesson for mocking me in front of my place,

[ʔuʃ   fiɛːbɛː   nɛbɔ   t'ɛ   daːm   dɔxtɔrɔvɪ]

už   hébé,   nebo   tě   dám   dochtorovi.
already get out of here, or   you   I'll give to doctor.

now get out of here, or I'll turn you over to my lawyer.

[ʔat'   t'ɪ   zaʒalujɛ   k‿ sɔːdu]

Ať̆   ti   zažaluje   k   sódu!
Let   you   he will take   to   court!

Let him take you to court!

(Znovu ji přetáhne.) (Again he hits her.)

Bystrouška: (nadzdvihne sukni) (she lifts up her skirt)

[tu   tɔt'   gambaːt͡ʃu   zɦɲlɛː   sɪrɔft͡ʃɛ   sɪrɔvɛː]

Tu   toť̆!   Gambáču   zhnilé,   syrovče syrové!
Here   look!   Arrogant one disgusting, brute   crude!

Look here! You disgusting jerk, vulgar brute!

Lesní havĕt':

[gambaːt͡ʃu   zfiɲɪlɛː   sɪrɔft͡ʃɛ   sɪrɔvɛː]

Gambáču   ⁷shnilé,   syrovče   syrové!
Arrogant one   disgusting,   brute   crude!

You disgusting jerk, vulgar brute!

Bystrouška: Lesní havĕt':

[t͡sɔ   mnɛ   mlaːt'iːʃ]   [t͡sɔ   ju   mlaːt'iːʃ]

Co   mne   mlátíš?   **Co   ju   mlátíš?**
Why   me   you hit?   Why   her   you hit?

Why are you hitting me?   *Why are you hitting her?*

Bystrouška:

[zavaziːm   t'ɪ   ʃpɪnaft͡ʃɛ   ʃpɪnavɛː   ʒɛ   mnɛ   klut͡ʃɛʃ]

Zavazím   ti,   špinavče   špinavé,   že   mne   klučeš?
Am I in the way   to you,   filth   dirty,   that   me   you hit?

Am I in your way, you dirty filth, that you beat me?

⁸see note

Lesní havět':

[zavaziː   t'ɪ   ʃpɪnaftʃɛ   ʃpɪnaveː]

Zavazí   ti,   špinavče   špinavé?
Is she in the way   to you,   filth   dirty?

Is she in your way, you dirty filth?

Bystrouška: Lesní havět':

[lɛs   jɛ   tak   vɛlkiː]   [lɛs   jɛ   tak   vɛlkiː]

Les   je   tak   velký,   **Les   je   tak   velký,**
Forest   is   so   big,   Forest   is   so   big,

The forest is so big,   *The forest is so big,*

Bystrouška:

[ʔa   fspɔmɛnɛ   sɪ   mɪlɔstpaːn]

a   vzpomene si   milostpán,
and   considers   lord,

and the lord decrees

[ʒɛ   ɲɪgdɔ   nɛsmiː   ʔɔkɔlɔvaː   ʔɔkɛn]

že   nikdo   nesmí   okolová   oken!
that   no one   may   hang around   window!

that no one may hang around his window!

Lesní havět':

[ʔa   ɲɪgdɔ   nɛsmiː   ʔɔkɔlɔvaː   ʔɔkɛn]

a   **nikdo**   **nesmí**   **okolová**   **oken!**
and   no one   may   hang around   window!

and no one may hang around his window!

Bystrouška:

[jaː   bɪx   t'ɛ   mɲɛla   daːt   k ‿ sɔːdu]

Já   **bych**   **tě**   **měla**   **dát**   **k**   **sódu!**
I   should   you   take   to put   to   court!

I should take you to court!

                                    Lesní havět':

[ʔalɛ gdɔ bɪ   sɛ   s‿tɛbɔu   mazal]   [dɛː fiɔ   k‿sɔːdu]

Ale   **kdo**   **by**   **se**   **s**   **tebou**   **mazal!**   **Dé**   **ho**   **k**   **sódu!**
But   who would   -   with you   get dirty!   Put   him   to   court!

But who would stoop to go near you!   *Take him to court!*

Bystrouška:

[tu   maːʃ   ɲɛt͡sɔ   ʒɛnskiːfiɔ]

Tu   **máš**   **něco**   **ženskýho,**
Here   you have   something   feminine,

Here's something feminine,

(Nadzdvihne oháňku.) (She lifts her tail.)
[ʔabɪs   vjɛd'ɛl   ʒɛ   su   ʔuznalaː]

abys   věděl,   že   su   uznalá.
so that   you would know   that I am appreciative.

so you may know I am appreciative.

(Odběhne na brdeček.)   (Jezevec vyjde z doupěte; rozhorleně.)
(She leaves a little pile.)   (The Badger runs out of his lair; furiously.)

Jezevec:

[ʔɔː jak   ˡsɛm ː mravɲɛ   rɔzɦɔŘt͡ʃɛn]

Ó, jak   jsem mravně   rozhořčen!
Oh, how   I am   morally   outraged!

Oh, how I am morally outraged!

[ʔɔpust'iːm   nɛvd'ɛt͡ʃnɛː   staːdɔ]

Opustím   nevděčné   stádo.
I'll abandon   ungrateful   herd.

I'll leave this ungrateful herd.

(Osuší slzu a vykročí s dýmkou pod paží do lesa.)
(He wipes away a tear and steps out with his pipe under his arm to the forest.)

(Bystrouška vítězoslavně vklouzne do opuštěného doupěte.)
(Bystrouška victoriously slips into the abandoned lair.)

Proměna   Scene change [Act II, scene ii]

(Hospodský hluk) (Inn noise)

Opona Curtain

(V hospodě „u Pásků"; panská světnice, vedle šenkovna)
(In the inn [9]"u Pásků;" men's sitting room, next to the bar)

Farář: (s tvářností jezevcovou vchází s dýmkou)
(with the Badger's appearance he enters with a pipe)

        (u stolu rechtor s revírníkem hrají v karty)
        (at the table the Schoolmaster plays cards with the Forester)
[ʔanɔ vɛ‿ straːɲɪ budɛ dalɛkɔ lɛːpɛ]

Ano,	**ve**	**Stráni**	**bude**	**daleko**	**lépe!**
Yes,	in	Stráň	it will be	far	better!

Yes, in [10]*Stráň it will be far better!*

Revírník:

[ʔɔːⁱ duːstɔⁱnɛː ʔɔː duːstɔⁱnɛː budɛmɛ miːt slavnɛː ʔɔdːdafkɪ]

Ój, důstojné! Ó,   důstojné, budeme mít slavné oddavky.
Oh, Reverend! Oh, Reverend, we will have glorious wedding.

Oh, Reverend! Oh, Reverend, we'll have a glorious wedding.

[mɪsliːm ʒɛ sɪ rɛxtɔřɪskɔ ɲɛjakaː ʔɔsɛdlala]

Myslím, že si rechtořisko   nějaká   osedlala.
I think that - little schoolmaster some female had control over.

I think some female has her sights on our Schoolmaster.

Farář:

[nɔn   dɛs   mulıjɛri   kɔrpus   tuum]

Non   des   mulieri   corpus   tuum!
Do not   give   to woman   body   your!

Non des mulieri corpus tuum!

Revírník:

[tı   pɔt'ɔːxlɛntʃɛ   pɔvjɛs   maːʃlı   jakɔu]

Ty   poťóchlenče,   pověz,   máš-li   jakou?
You   sly one,   say,   have you-if   some woman?

You sly devil, tell us if you have some woman?

[fʃak   jaː   tɔ   s ‿ tɛbɛ   dɔstanu]

Však   já   to   z   tebe   dostanu!
But   I   it   from   you   will get!

But I'll get it out of you!

[biːvalɔ   biːvalɔ   daːvnɔ   ʔuʃ   nɛɲiː]

Bývalo,   bývalo,   dávno   už   není,
It used to be,   it used to be,   long ago   by now   it isn't,

There was a time, there was a time, it's no longer,

[11]see note

[tɔbjɛ　　jɛn　　vɛruŋkɔ　　xt'ɛlɔ　sɛ　　bd'ɛɲiː]

tobě　**jen,**　**Verunko,**　**chtělo se**　**bdění;**
to you　only,　Verunka,　felt like　staying up awake;

when you, Verunka, felt like staying up late;

[na‿svjɛt'ɛ　trat'iː　sɛ　fʃɛt͡skɔ　　ʔa　　mɲɛɲiː]

na　**světě**　**tratí**　**se**　**všecko**　**a**　**mění,**
on　world　disappears　everything　and　it changes,

in the world everything disappears and changes,

[mɔdřiːn　sɛ　zɛlɛnal　　kvjɛtɛn　bɪl　　gdɪsɪ]

modřín　**se zelenal,**　**květen**　**byl**　**kdysi,**
larch　turned green,　May　was　at one time,

the larch turned green, it was May once,

[vɛruŋka　　sɛ　staːrla　　mɔdřiːn　jɛ　　lɪsiː]

Verunka　**se**　**stárla,**　¹²**modřín je**　**lysý.**
Verunka　grew old,　larch　is　bare.

Verunka has grown old, the larch is bare.

[ktɛrak　　jiː　　nɪɲiː　ʔas　　　　pɔ‿leːtɛx　řiːkaː]

Kterak　**jí**　**nyní**　**as**　　　**po**　**létech**　**říká?**
How　to her　now　perhaps　after　years　he says?

How does he call her now after so many years?

Rechtor: (vyčitavě) (reproachfully)

[panɛ fɔR̂tɛ]

Pane   fořte!
Mr.   forester!

Mr. Forester!

Revírník:

[ml̩t͡ʃiː   gdɪʃ   pɔtkaː   ɦɔ]

Mlčí,   když   potká   ho,
She's silent   when   she encounters   him,

She's silent when she meets him,

[ml̩t͡ʃiː   gdɪʃ   pɔtkaː   ɦɔ   vɛrɔnɪka]

mlčí,   když   potká   ho,   [13]Veronika.
she's silent   when   she encounters   him,   Veronika.

she's silent when she meets him, Veronika.

Rechtor:

[paːɲɪ   fɔR̂t'ɪ   miːvajiː   nɛʃt'ɛst'iː   ɦɔrʃiː]

Páni   fořti   mívají   neštěstí   horší!
Mister   foresters   have had   misfortune   worse!

Foresters have had worse luck!

[slɪʃɛl ˡsɛm ʒɛ ˡstɛ sɪ dɔnɛsl̩ lɪʃku dɔmuː]

Slyšel jsem, že jste si donesl lišku domů.

| I heard | that you | yourself | brought | vixen | home. |

I heard that you brought a vixen home with you.

[jak sɛ vaːm vɪdaři̩la]

Jak se vám vydařila?
How - to you she succeeded?

How did she turn out for you?

Revírník: (dopáleně) (angrily)

[deˡtɛ mɪ s‿ ɲiː pɔkɔˡ ta mnɛ pɔtvɔra dɔstala]

Dejte mi s ní pokoj! Ta mne potvora dostala!
Give to me with her peace! That me bitch got the better of!

I don't want to talk about her! That bitch got the better of me!

[raːt ˡsɛm sɛ bɛstɪjɛ splɛl lɛpʃiː nɛmɪslɛt]

Rád jsem se ¹⁴bestie splel! Lepší nemyslet!
Glad I am - bitch rid of! Better not to think!

I'm glad I'm rid of the bitch! Better not to think about it!

[zrɔvna   jak   t͡ʃlɔvjɛk]

Zrovna,   jak   člověk!
Just   like   man!

Just like a man!

[jak   zat͡ʃnɛ   kaɲkɔvat   tak   zɣlɔːpnɛ]

Jak   začne   kaňkovat,   tak   zhlópne.
How   he begins to be in heat, so   he becomes stupid.

The moment he goes into heat, he becomes stupid.

[fʃɪmɲɛtɛ   sɪ   tɔt'   rɛxtɔra]

Všimněte si   toť̌   rechtora.
Take heed of   to be sure schoolmaster.

Just look at the Schoolmaster.

[nɛɲiː tɔ   mɔːdrɛː   t͡ʃlɔvjɛk]

Není to   módré   člověk?
Isn't he   wise   man?

Isn't he a wise man?

[ʔa   ft͡ʃɪl   miːstɔ   vaːm   maʒɛ   ʔɛsɔ   mɲɛ]

A   včil   místo   vám   maže   eso   mě.
And now   instead of to you   passes ace to me.

And now instead of to you he's passed an ace to me.

(vejde otec Pásek) (the innkeeper Pásek enters)

[ʔɔ rɛxtɔrɛ   kantɔrɛ   filɔːpnɛʃ]

O, rechtore,   kantore,   hlópneš.
Oh, schoolmaster, teacher,   you're getting stupid.

Oh, Schoolmaster, teacher, you're getting stupid.

Farář:

[nɔn   dɛs   mulijɛri   kɔrpus   tuum]

Non   des   mulieri   corpus   tuum.
Do not give   to woman   body   your!

Non des mulieri corpus tuum.

Revírník:

[t͡ʃɛrta   rɔzumiːm]

Čerta   rozumím!
Of devil   I understand!

The hell I understand!

Farář:

[tɔʃ   t͡ʃɛskɪ]

Tož   česky:
Then   in Czech:

Translation:

[nɛdaːʃ   ʒɛɲɛ   t'ɛla   svɛːɦɔ]

„ **Nedáš   ženě   těla   svého.** "
"Do not give   to a woman   body   your."

"Do not give to a woman your body."

[15]see note

Revírník:

[gdɪbɪ   tɔ   bɪla   ʔaspɔɲ   mɪslɪvɛtska: lat'ɪna]

Kdyby to   byla   aspoň   myslivecká   [16]latina.
  If it had been   at least   gamekeeper's   Latin.

If only it had been gamekeeper's Latin.

Farář:

[nɛdaːʃ   ʒɛɲɛ   t'ɛla   svɛːɦɔ]

„ **Nedáš   ženě   těla   svého.** "
"Do not give   to a woman   body   your."

"Do not give to a woman your body."

Revírník:

[baʒɛ   ftʃɪl   ʔuʃ   nɛ]

Baže,   včil   už   ne,
Sure,   now   already not,

Sure, it's too late now,

(nadzvedá šosy rechtorovi) (he lifts the Schoolmaster's coat-tails)

[t͡ʃɪ   řiːkaːtɛ   tɛːtɔ   ʔɔstriːft͡sɛ   tʼɛlɔ]

či   **říkáte**   **této**   [17]**ostrývce**   **tělo?**
or   do you say   this   ladder   body?

or do you call this stick a body?

[kɔstr̩batɛː   jak   lɔut͡ʃ]

[18]**Kostrbaté**   **jak**   **louč.**
   Knobby   like   stick of kindling.

Knobby like a stick of kindling.

Rechtor:

[bɔdeⁱtʼ   bɪstɛ   nɛʒdʼaːraːlɪ]

Bodejt'   **byste**   **nežd'áráli.**
You bet   you would stop teasing.

Would you stop kidding.

(Jde k oknu.) (He goes toward the window.)

[19]see note

[kɔɦɔut   spiːvaː   t͡ʃas   dɔmuː   jiːt]

Kohout   **zpívá,**   **čas**   **domů**   **jít!**
Rooster   sings,   time   home   to go!

The cock is crowing, it's time to go home!

(Béře klobouk, platí.) (He takes his hat, he pays.)

Revírník:

[sɛtsakrapɛs   nɛx   kɔɦɔːta   kɔɦɔːtɛm]

Setsakrapes!	**Nech**	**kohóta**	**kohótem!**
Good heavens!	Leave	rooster	to rooster!

Good heavens! Let the cock be a cock!

[prɔ‿ jɛdnɔɦɔ   pɛtr̩   krɪsta   zrad'ɪl]

Pro	**jednoho**	**Petr**	**Krista**	**zradil.**
For	one	Peter	Christ	betrayed.

Peter betrayed Christ for one.

Rechtor: (odchází z hospody) (he leaves the inn)

[z‿ bɔɦɛm]

S Bohem!
Farewell!

Farewell!

Pásek: (šeptá faráři do ucha) (he whispers in the Pastor's ear)

[duːstɔⁱnɛː]

Důstojné!
Reverend!

Reverend!

[duːstɔˈnɛː ˈidɔu   k‿vaːm   vaʃɪ   nɔviː   naːmjɛmɲiːt͡sɪ]

Důstojné, jdou   k   vám   vaši   noví   námjemníci.
Reverend, they go   to   you   your   new   tenants.

Reverend, your new tenants are coming for you.

Farář:

[nat͡ʃ   fspɔmiːnaːtɛ]

Nač   vzpomínáte!
Why   do you remember!

Why do you remind me!

(Rychle béře klobouk a odchází.) (Quickly he takes his hat and leaves.)

(Divoká společnost ze šenkovny vtírá se do panské světnice.)
(A wild group from the bar intrudes on the gentlemen's sitting-room.)

(Hluk hospodský) (Noise of the inn)

[20]Sbor:

[mɪlɔstpaːn   mɪlɔstpaːn   mɪlɔstpaːn   mɪlɔstpaːn]

Milostpán! Milostpán!   Milostpán!   Milostpán!
Lord!   Lord!   Lord!   Lord!

Lord! Lord! Lord! Lord!

Revírník: (podnapilý) (tipsy)

[dɔmuː   prɔ ‿   tɛn   ʃɲupɛt͡s   tvɛːɦɔ   spaɲiː]

Domů?	Pro	ten	²¹šňupec	tvého	spaní?
Home?	For	that	bit	of your	sleep?

Home! Just for a bit of sleep?

[ʔɔ   rɛxtɔrɛ   jɪdaːʃɪ]   [zdaː sɛ   mɪ]

O,	rechtore,	Jidáši!		Zdá	se	mi,
Oh,	schoolmaster,	Judas!		It seems	to me	

Oh, Schoolmaster, you Judas!   *It seems to me*

[ʒɛ   pR̝et͡sɛ   prɔdaːʃ   svɛː   starɛː   kɔstˈɪ   ʒɛnskɛː]

že	přece	prodáš	své	staré	kosti	ženské,
that	after all	you'll sell	your	old	bones	to woman,

that you'll sell your old bones to a woman

[miːstɔ   ʒidɔvɪ   praviːʃ   ʒɛ   nɛ]

místo	židovi?		Pravíš,	že	ne?
instead of	to Jew?		You say	that	no?

instead of to a Jew? Do you deny it?

²²see note

(k Páskovi) (to Pásek)

[f ‿ pɔtu   tvaːr̝ɛ   jiːstʼɪ   budɛʃ   xlɛːp   svuːⁱ]

„V	potu	tváře	jísti	budeš	chléb	svůj.“
"In	sweat	of face	to eat	you will	bread	your."

"In the sweat of thy face shalt thou eat thy bread."

[23]see note

[ʔalɛ ʔɔ ‿ pɪtʼiː   ʔaɲɪ   muk   ʒɛ   nɛ]

Ale	o	pití	ani	muk!	Že	ne?
But	about	drinking	not	word!	That	no?

But about drinking not a word! Isn't that so?

[gdɪbɪ bɪl   ɦɔspɔdʼɪn   ʔudʼɛlal   ʔaspɔɲ   zmɪnɛt͡ʃku]

Kdyby byl	Hospodin	udělal	aspoň	zminečku,
If He had	Lord	made	at least	small mention

If the Lord had made at least some mention

[ʒɛ   piːtʼɪ   budɛm   z ‿ baːzɲiː   ʔa   tR̝ɛsɛɲiːm]

že	píti	budem	s	bázní	a	třesením.
that	to drink	we will	with	fear	and	trembling.

that we will drink with fear and trembling . . .

[praviːʃ   ʒɛ   nɛ   prɔtɔ   panɛ   paːsku   jɛʃt'ɛ   jɛdnu]

Pravíš,   že   ne?   Proto,   pane Pásku,   ještě   jednu!
You say that   no?   Therefore, mister Pásek,   still   one!

Do you deny it? So, Mr. Pásek, another one!

[ʒɛ   nɛ]

Že   ne?
That   no?

Isn't that so?

Pásek:

[ʔalɛ s ⌣ tɔu   lɪʃkɔu   tɔ   sɪ   jɛʃt'ɛ   vspɔmɛnɛtɛ   na ⌣ naːs]

Ale   s   tou   liškou   to   si   ještě   vzpomenete   na   nás.
But with that   vixen   it   -   still   you recall   to   us.

But about that vixen—you still recall what we said.

Revírník: (vybuchne) (he explodes)

[dɔ ⌣ firɔma   nɛmaːm   t͡sɔ   vspɔmiːnat]

Do   hroma,   nemám,   co   vzpomínat!
To   thunder,   I don't have   what   to remember!

Damn it, I don't have anything to recall!

[utɛkla   utɛkla   ʔa   jɛ]

Utekla!   Utekla   a   je!
She ran away!   She ran away   and   it is!

She ran away! She ran away and that's it!

[jaː   jɪ   ɦlɛdat   nɛbudu]

Já   ji   hledat   nebudu!
I   her   to look for will not!

I won't look for her!

[zuːstaːveⁱtɛ   s ‿ paːnɛm   bɔɦɛm]

Zůstávejte   s   pánem   bohem!   (odchází) (he leaves)
Stay   with Lord   God!

Goodbye!

Opona Curtain

[The following stage directions occur in the orchestral score, but not in
the piano/vocal score, two measures before rehearsal 24:

(Pásek sbírá peníz utržený.) (Pásek picks up the money he gained.)

(Přehodí pušku a odejde vrávoravě.)
(He [the Forester] throws his rifle on his shoulder and leaves teeter-
ing.)]

Opona Curtain

Proměna: Scene change: [Act II, scene iii]

(Les; nalevo cestička do vrchu, podél plot s kvetoucí slunečnicí. Noc; měsíční světlo)

(Forest; on the left a little path leads upwards, along a fence with a blooming sunflower. Night; moonlight)

Rechtor: (vykračuje po cestičce) (he ambles along the little path)

[but'tɔ   maːm   t'ɛʒɪʃt'ɛ   pɔfiːblɪvɛː]

Bud'to	**mám**	**těžiště**	**pohyblivé,**
Either	I have	center of gravity	moving,

Either I have a shifting center of gravity,

[nɛbɔ sɛ tɔtʃiː   zɛmɲɛ   ʔɔd ‿ zaːpadu k ‿ viːxɔdu]

nebo	**se**	**točí**	**země**	**od**	**západu**	**k**	**východu.**
or	it	turns	earth	from	west	to	east.

or the earth is turning from the west to the east.

[t͡sɔsɪ   dnɛs   nɛɲiː   f‿ pɔřaːtku]

Cosi	**dnes**	**není**	**v**	**pořádku.**
Something	today	is not	in	order.

Something today isn't right.

[bɪlɔ   mɪ   tř ɛba   nɔt͡sɔvat]

Bylo	**mi**	**třeba**	**nocovat**
Was it	to me	necessary	to spend the night

Was it necessary for me to spend the night

[v‿ ɦɔspɔd'ɛ   u ‿ t͡sɪziːx   lɪd'iː]

v	**hospodě**	**u**	**cizích**	**lidí?**
in	pub	with	strange	people?

in the pub with strange people?

[bɪlɔ   mɪ   tŘɛba   nɛspat]

Bylo	**mi**	**třeba**	**nespat,**
Was it	for me	necessary	not to sleep,

Was it necessary for me to stay awake,

[gdɪʃ   spiː   t͡sɛliː   svjɛt]

když	**spí**	**celý**	**svět?**
when	sleeps	whole	world?

when the whole world sleeps?

[pɔtŘɛbujɪ   jaː   ɦlɛdat   t͡sɛstu   vɛ‿ tmɲɛ   dɔmuː]

Potřebuji	**já**	**hledat**	**cestu**	**ve**	**tmě**	**domů?**
I need	I	to look for	path	in	dark	home?

Do I need to look for a path home in the dark?

[ʔa   biːt   raːt   ʒɛ   sɪ   nɛvɪvr̥tnu   nɔɦu   nɛp   ruku]

A	**být**	**rád,**	**že**	**si**	**nevyvrtnu**	**nohu**	**neb**	**ruku?**
And	to be	glad	that	I don't sprain		leg	or	arm?

And be glad that I don't sprain a leg or an arm?

(Zastaví se) (He pauses)

[zatra͡tsɛnaː t͡sɛsta zas jɪ vɪbral dɛːʃt']

Zatracená   cesta!   Zas   ji   vybral   déšť!
Damned   road!   Again it   cleared rain!

Damned road! The rain has washed it away again!

[gdɪbɪx nɛmɲel fiɔlɛ t͡ʃɪ ʔɔpɔrɪ vuːbɛt͡s]

Kdybych neměl   hole,   či   opory   vůbec,
If I did not have stick, or   supports at all,

If I didn't have a stick, or any support,

[dɔmuː bɪx sɛ nɛdɔstal]

domů   bych se nedostal.
home   I would not get.

I wouldn't make it home.

[dvjɛ nɔfiɪ ʔa fiuːl tɔ ⁱsɔu tR̥ɪ ʔɔpjɛɲiː bɔdɔvɛː]

Dvě nohy a   hůl   to   jsou tři   opěrní   bodové.
Two legs and stick those are three supporting points.

Two legs and a stick, those are my three points of support.

[t'ɛmɪtɔ   tŘ̌ɛmɪ   bɔdɪ   maːm   nɛⁱpravɪdɛlɲɛⁱʃiː stɔjatɔst]

Těmito   třemi   body   mám   nejpravidelnější stojatost.
With these   three   points   I have   the most steady   stability.

With these three points I have the most secure stability.

[nɔ   skusiːm   tɔ   bɛz ‿   ɦɔlɛ]

No,   zkusím   to   bez   hole.
Well,   I'll try   it   without   stick.

Well, I'll try it without a stick.

(Smýkne sebou, tu dopředu, to dozadu.)
(He slides, now forwards, now backwards.)

[mɔrdɪjɛː]   [24]see note

Mordié! (upadne) (he falls)
Damn!

Damn!

(Bystrouška vběhne za slunečnicí.)
(Bystrouška runs in behind the sunflower.)

(Rechtor se udiveně zadívá na slunečnici.)
(The Schoolmaster stares, amazed, at the sunflower.)

[stakːkatɔ]

Staccato!
Staccato!

Staccato!

(Zarazí se, zvedne ukazováček do výše.)
(He stops short and holds up high his index finger.)

²⁵see note

[flaʒɪjɔletːtɔ]

Flažioletto!
Flagioletto!

²⁶*Flagioletto!*

²⁷see note

(Van větru; slunečnice se zatřese tajemně.)
(The wind blows; the sunflower shakes mysteriously.)

(pozvedne oči úžasem) (he lifts his eyes in astonishment)

[ʔɔː ʔɔː terɪŋkɔ]

Ó, ó Terynko!
Oh, oh Terynka!

Oh, oh Terynka!

[gdɪbɪx   bɪl   vjed'el   ʒe   vaːs   tu   pɔtkaːm]

Kdybych   byl   věděl,   že ²⁸vás   tu   potkám,
    If I had known   that you   here   encounter,

If I had known that I would meet you here,

[bɪl   bɪx   daːvnɔ   ʔɔpust'ɪl   ʔɔbʒerɲiːkɪ   ʔɔba]

byl   bych   dávno   opustil   obžerníky   oba.
  I would   long ago have deserted drunkards   both.

I would have deserted those two drunkards long ago.

[vɪ   mnɛ   mɪlujɛtɛ   ʔɔː   prɔmluftɛ]

Vy   mne   milujete?   Ó   promluvte!
You   me   do you love?   Oh   speak!

Do you love me? Oh speak!

(Záhadná bytost vrtí hlavou.) (The enigmatic creature shakes its head.)

[jaː   vaːs   naːvɪd'iːm   ʔuʃ   lɛːta   lɛtɔut͡siː]

Já   vás   návidím,   už   léta   letoucí,
I   you   love,   already   ages and ages,

I've loved you for ages and ages,

[29]see note

[vaːʃ   ʔɔsut   jɛ   v‿   mɪːx   rukɔu   ʔa   t͡ʃɛkaːm   t͡sɔ   ʔɔtpɔviːtɛ]

váš   osud je v   mých rukou a   čekám, co   odpovíte!
your   fate   is in   my   hands and I await what you'll answer!

[30]*your fate is in my hands, and I await your answer!*

[ʔɔtpust'tɛ   muʒɪ   xabɛːmu   fiɔřiːt͡siːmu   laːskɔːu]

Odpusťte   muži   chabému,   hořícímu   láskou!
Forgive   man   weak,   burning   with love!

Forgive a weak man, burning with love!

[puːᶦdu   za‿vaːmɪ   puːᶦdu   sɛvru   vaːs   dɔ‿svɛː naːrutʃɛ]

Půjdu   za   vámi,   půjdu.   Sevru   vás   do   své   náruče.
I will go to   you,   I will go. I'll hug you   to   my   arms.

I'll go to you, I'll go. I'll hold you in my arms.

(Slunečnice se odkloní od plotu.)
(The sunflower sways away from the fence.)

(k sobě) (to himself)
[ʔafia   ʔuʃ   mɪ   d'ɛlaː   miːstɔ]

Aha,   už   mi   dělá   místo.
Aha,   already   to me   she makes   space.

Aha, already she's making room for me.

[tʃɛfiɔ   sɛ   jɛʃt'ɛ   dɔʒɪju]

Čeho   se   ještě   dožiju. . .
What   -   still   will I live to see. . .

What experience lies ahead?. . .

(Vír vášní jím zalomcuje, hůl vypadne mu z ruky; rozběhne se k plotu, přemete se kozelcem, až plot zapraská.)
(A whirl of passion overtakes him, the stick falls from his hand; he starts to run toward the fence, somersaults, and the fence makes a cracking sound.)

(Bystrouška mihne se od slunečnice; ukryje se v křoví.)
(Bystrouška zooms away from the sunflower; she hides in the bushes.)

Farář: (přichází z dola) (he comes in from below)

[pɔmɲɪ   ʔabɪz bɪl   dɔbriːm : muʒɛm]

„**Pomni,**   **abys byl**   **dobrým   mužem!**"
"Remember   that you should be good   man!"

"Remember that you should be a good man!"

(Rechtor se vrtí za plotem.)
(The Schoolmaster trembles behind the fence.)

[ɦrɔmɛ   s ‿ ktɛrɛːɦɔ jɛ   tɔ   klasɪka]

Hrome,   z   kterého   je   to   klasika?
Damn,   from   which   is   that classic?

Damn, what classic is that from?

(Zapaluje a sedne příliš náhle.)
(He lights his pipe and sits down too abruptly.)

[nɛfiɔřiː   t͡sɔ   ⁱsɛm   sɛ   tak   nasɛdaːval]

Nehoří!   Co   jsem   se   tak   nasedával!
It doesn't burn! What I did   -   so   sit down!

It won't burn! I used to sit here like this!

[jaː mladiːm studɛntɛm]

Já   mladým studentem
I   young   student

I was a young student

[ʔɔna t͡sɔpaːnɛk mɲɛla jakɔ zɛ‿ zlata]

ona   **copánek**   **měla**   **jako** **ze** **zlata**
she   braids   she had   like   from   gold,

and she had braids like gold,

[ʔa ʔɔt͡ʃɪma sɛ dʼiːvala nɛvɪnɲɛ]

a   **očima**   **se**   **dívala**   **nevinně,**
and   with eyes   she looked   innocently,

and she gazed with innocent eyes,

(Bystrouščiny oči svítí z křoví.)
(Bystrouška's eyes shine from the bushes.)

[nɛxaːpavjɛ]

nechápavě.
uncomprehendingly.

uncomprehendingly.

[daːvnɔ jɛ tɔmu pak bɪlɔ fʃɛmu kɔnɛt͡s]

Dávno   **je**   **tomu.** [31]**Pak**   **bylo**   **všemu**   **konec.**
Long ago   is   it.   Then   it was   everything end.

It was long ago. Then everything came to an end.

[ʔɔtʃɪ jakɔ tuːɲ v ‿ ɦlɔːupt͡sɛ ʔɔblɔɦa nɛbɛskaː]

Oči jako tůň, v   hloubce   obloha   nebeská,
Eyes like pool, in   depth   sky   heavenly,

Eyes like a pool, in their depths a heavenly sky,

[ʔa   jɛʃt'ɛ   ɦlɔubjɛjɪ]

a   ještě   hlouběji,
and   still   deeper,

and still deeper,

[ʔa jɛʃt'ɛ ɦlɔubjɛjɪ zrada ʔɔʃɛmɛtnaː jak slɪskɛː dnɔ]

a   ještě   hlouběji zrada ošemetná jak slizké dno!
and still   deeper betrayal deceitful like slimy lake bottom!

and still deeper wicked betrayal like a slimy lake bottom!

[z ‿ r̝ɛzɲɪt͡skiːm   tɔvarɪʃɛm]

S   řeznickým   tovaryšem!
With   butcher's   apprentice!

With the butcher's apprentice!

[ʔa   mɲɛ   ʔɔbvɪɲɔvalɪ   panaːt͡ʃka ʔalɔⁱzɛ]

A   mě   obviňovali,   panáčka   Alojze!
And   me   they blamed,   young priest   Alois!

And they blamed me, the seminarian Alois!

[32]see note

(výsměšně) (scornfully)   (Bystrouščiny oči zasvitnou opět.)
                            (Bystrouška's eyes gleam again.)

[kɔt͡ʃɪt͡ʃka na ‿ jiːvjɛ   zuzana   t͡snɔstnaː v ‿ laːzɲɪ]

[33]**Kočička, na   jívě.   Zuzana   ctnostná   v   lázni.**
Catkin,   on pussy willow. Susannah virtuous   in   bath.

Innocent as a lamb. Virtuous Susannah.

[ʔɔt ː tɛː   dɔbɪ]
Od   té   doby
Since that   time

Since then

[nɛmɲɛl ˈsɛm t͡ʃɪstɛːfiɔ   pɔfilɛdu ʔaɲɪ prɔ ‿ jɛd'ɪnɔːu]

neměl jsem čistého   pohledu ani   pro   jedinou!
 I have not of clean   glance   even for a single woman!

*I haven't looked at any woman without having dirty thoughts
about her!*

[pR̝ɛʃlɔ   ﬀɛt͡skɔ]

Přešlo   všecko.
It has passed   everything.

It's all over.

[tɛt' stɔjiːm jakɔ smɛtaːk f ͜ kɔut'ɛ]

Ted' stojím jako smeták v koutě.
Now I stand like broom in corner.

Now I'm left standing like a broom in a corner.

[mɛmnɛstɔː ʔanɛːr ʔagatɔs ʔɛɪnaɪ]

„**Memnesthó anér agathos einai.**"
34„Memnesthó anér agathos einai."

"Memnesthó anér agathos einai."

(radostně) (joyfully)
[tɔ jɛ pR͡ɛt͡sɛ s ͜ ksɛnɔfɔntɔvɪ ʔanabaːzɛ]

To je přece z Xenofontovy Anábáse!
That is yet from 35Xenophon's Anabasis!

But of course, it's from Xenophon's Anabasis!

Revírník: (za jevištěm) (behind the scene)

(Bystrouška chvatně přeběhne.) (Bystrouška hurriedly runs away.)
[kujɔːnɛ ʔuʃ t'ɛ ʒɛnu]

36**Kujóne!   Už   tě   ženu!**
Smart ass! Already you   I catch!

Smart ass! I've got you now!

Rechtor: (sbírá se se země) (pulls himself up from the ground)
Farář: (sbírá se se země) (pulls himself up from the ground)

[prɔ‿ bɔfia tadɪ   nɛsmiːm   zuːstat]

Pro Boha! Tady   nesmím   zůstat!
For   God!   Here   I may not stay!

Good Heavens! I can't stay here!

[tɛn   ː   nɛrɔzumiː]

Ten   nerozumí,
That one   doesn't understand

He doesn't understand

[ʒɛ   jɛ   t͡ʃlɔvjɛk   kŘɛxkaː   naːdɔba]

že   je   člověk   křehká   nádoba!
that   is   man   fragile   vessel!

that man is a fragile vessel!

(Rechtor přeleze plot a rychle odvrávorá.)
(The Schoolmaster climbs over the fence and quickly staggers away.)

Revírník: (za scénou:) (behind the scene:)

[lɪʃka]

Liška!
Vixen!

The vixen!

(Farář odbíhá opačným směrem.)
(The Pastor runs away in the opposite direction.)

(☉ Rána z pušky) (Shot from the rifle)   (☉ druhá rána) (Second shot)

[37]see note

(Vystupuje z lesa s puškou.) (He comes out from the forest with his rifle.)

[na‿ mɪnut   fiɔd'ɪnɪ   ʒɛ   tɔ   bɪla   naʃa   lɪʃka]

Na	**minut**	**hodiny,**	**že**	**to**	**byla**	**naša**	**liška!**
At	minute	of hour	that	that	was	our	vixen!

I'd bet anything that was our vixen!

Opona Curtain

Proměna   Scene change [Act II, scene iv]

[38]see note

Sbor: (Za scénou) (Behind the scene)

[ʔa]

A

Ah!

Opona. Curtain.

(Doupě Bystroušky. Letní, měsíčná noc.)
(Bystrouška's lair. Summer, moonlit night.)

(Bystrouška leží, čenich na předních tlapkách.)
(Bystrouška is lying down, her snout on her front paws.)

(Křoví zapraští.) (The bushes make a crackling sound.)

Bystrouška: (třese se po celém těle) (she trembles throughout her whole body)

[bɔːʒɪŋku   tɛn   jɛ   ɦɛsskɛː]

Bóžinku,   ten   je   hezké!
Goodness,   that one   is   handsome!

Wow, he's handsome!

(Pohlcuje Lišáka očima.) (She devours the Fox with her eyes.)

(Z mlází zasvitnou žluté, žhavé oči Lišákovy.)
(From the undergrowth gleam the yellow, glowing eyes of the Fox.)

[tɛn   jɛ   ɦɛsskɛː]

Ten   je   [39]hezké!
That one   is   handsome!

He's handsome!

Lišák: (vystoupí uhlazeně) (he appears, mannerly)

[pɔlɛkala   ⁱstɛ   sɛ   slɛt͡ʃnɔ]

[40]Polekala   jste se,   slečno?
  Were you startled,   miss?

Were you startled, miss?

Bystrouška: (nevinně) (innocently)

[nɛʔɛ nɛʔɛ]

[41]**Nee!   Nee!**
No!   No!

No! No!

Lišák:

[tadɪ   ʔasɪ   ɦɲiːzd'ɪjɔu   ftaːt͡ʃtsɪ]

Tady   asi   **[42]hnízdijou   ftáčci?**
Here   perhaps   are nesting   birds?

Perhaps there are birds nesting here?

Bystrouška:	Lišák:
(skromně) (modestly)	
[baːt']	[ʔalɛ ft͡ʃɪl jɛ jɪx tu maːlɔ]

Bát̆!	**Ale včil je jich tu málo.**
Yes!	But now is of them here few.

| *Yes!* | *But now there are few of them here.* |

Bystrouška:

[baːt' jaː tɔtɔk mɪstɛt͡ʃkɔ dɔbr̝ɛ znaːm]

Bát̆,   já   totok   mistečko   dobře   znám,
Yes,   I   this   little place   well   I know,

Yes, I know this little place well,

[biːvaːm tɔt' nɛdalɛkɔ]

bývám toť nedaleko;
I live   here   not far;

I don't live far away from here;

[vɪʃla ⁱsɛm sɪ tutɔt' na ‿ prɔxaːsku]

vyšla jsem si tutoť na procházku,
I stepped out   here   for   walk,

I stepped out here for a walk,

[prɔtɔʒɛ mɲɛ straʃɲɛ bɔliː ɦlava]

protože mě strašně bolí hlava.
because   me   terribly   hurts   head.

because I have a terrible headache.

Lišák:

[tɔʃ dɔvɔltɛ prɔsiːm ʔabɪx vaːz dɔprɔvɔd'ɪl]

Tož dovolte, prosím, abych vás doprovodil.
Then allow,   please,   that I should you   accompany.

Then allow me, please, to accompany you.

[ft͡ʃɪl   zasɛ   mɪslɪft͡sɪ   lɔzɪjɔː   pɔ ‿ lɛsiːx]

Včil   zase   myslivci   lozijó   po   lesích,
Now   again   gamekeepers   prowl   through   woods,

Now the gamekeepers are prowling again in the woods,

[ʔa   gdɪʃ   jɛ   jɛdɛn   tak   zamɪʃlɛnɛː]

a   když   je   jeden   tak   zamyšlené,
and   if   is   one   so   lost in thought,

and if one is too lost in thought,

[lɛfkɔ   bɪ   pR̝ɪʃɛl   k ‿ ʔuːrazu]

[43]**lefko   by   přišel   k   úrazu!**
easily   would   come   to   injury!

he could be easily hurt!

Bystrouška: (zajíkavě) (falteringly)

[gdɪʃ   budɛtɛ   tak   lasskavɛː]

Když   budete   tak   [44]laskavé. . .
If   you will be   so   kind. . .

If you will be so kind . . .

Lišák: (chvatně) (rapidly)

[ʔɔffɛm   nɛbudɛlɪ   mat'ɪŋka   sɛ   ɦɲɛvat]

Ovšem,   nebude-li   matinka   se hněvat.
Of course,   she will not-if   mother   be angry.

Of course, if your mother will not be angry.

Bystrouška:

[ʔɔː nɛʔɛ jaː ⁱsɛm daːvnɔ   samɔstatnaː]

Ó,   nee!   Já   jsem   dávno   samostatná.
Oh   no!   I   am   a long time   independent.

Oh, no! I've been on my own for a long time.

Lišák: (pro sebe) (to himself)

[samɔstatnaː]

Samostatná?
Independent!

On her own?

Bystrouška:

[maːm   ʔajɪ   svuːⁱ   duːm]

Mám   **aji**   **svůj**   **dům.**
I have   even   my   house.

I even have my own house.

[ʔɔtkaːzal   mɪ   jeⁱ   striːt͡s   jɛzɛvet͡s]

Odkázal   **mi**   **jej**   **strýc**   **jezevec.**
He bequeathed to me   it   neighbor   badger.

My neighbor Badger bequeathed it to me.

Lišák: (s nelíčeným obdivem) (with genuine admiration)

[majɪtɛlka   dɔmu]

Majitelka   **domu?**
Owner   of house?

The owner of a house?

Bystrouška:

[ʔa   v ‿ mɪslɪvɲɛ   biːvala   ⁱsɛm   jakɔ   dɔma]

A   **v**   **myslivně**   **bývala**   **jsem**   **jako**   **doma.**
And   in   lodge   I used to be   like   at home.

And the Forester's lodge used to be home for me.

Lišák: (s údivem se uklání) (he bows in astonishment)

[v ‿ mɪslɪvɲɛ]

V   myslivně?
In   lodge?

In the Forester's lodge?

Bystrouška: (přešlapuje) (shuffling her feet)

[vɪrɔstla ˈsɛm tam | maːm lɪtskɛː vɪxɔvaːɲiː]

Vyrostla jsem   tam.   Mám   lidské   vychování.
  I grew up   there.   I have   human   upbringing.

I grew up there. I have a human upbringing.

[45](tlumeně) (quietly)
[kradla ˈsɛm]

Kradla jsem!
I stole!

I was a thief!

[jɛdnɔːu jɛʃtˈɛ mraːs mnɛ tɛtˈ pR̝ɛbiːɦaː xɪtlɪ   mnɛ]

Jednou, ještě mráz mne teď přebíhá, chytli   mne!
Once,   still   frost   me   now   runs down, they caught me!

Once—I still shiver thinking about it—they caught me!

[ʔalɛ lɪʃka sɛ ʔumiː braːɲɪt]

Ale liška se umí bránit!
But vixen herself knows how to defend!

But a vixen knows how to defend herself!

[ʔa takɛː sɛ ʔubraːɲiː]

A také se ubrání.
And also herself she defends successfully.

And so she does defend herself successfully.

[ʔumiːm ʔaspɔɲ jazɪk vɪplazɪt nɔ dɔmlaːt'ɪlɪ mnɛ]

Umím aspoň jazyk vyplazit! No, domlátili mne.
I know how at least tongue to stick out! Well, they beat me.

I at least know how to stick out my tongue! Well, they beat me.

[kus ʔɔfiaːɲkɪ ⁱsɛm strat'ɪla mɪslɪvɛts slɪbɔval]

Kus oháňky jsem ztratila. Myslivec sliboval:
Piece of tail I lost. Gamekeeper vowed:

I lost a piece of my tail. The gamekeeper vowed:

[ʔaɲɪ sɛ nɛptɛːtɛ jak jaː ju dɔbɪju]

„Ani se neptéte, jak já ju dobiju!
"Even don't you ask, how I her will finish off!

"Don't even ask how I'll beat her!

[ʔaʃ   padnɛ]

Až   padne,
When   she drops,

When she drops,

[vɪpaːraːm   jiː   tɛn   ɦr̩tan   ml̩snɛː]

vypárám   jí   ten   hrtan   mlsné
I'll slit   of her   that   pharynx   sweet-toothed

I'll slit that sweet-toothed throat of hers

[ʔa   tɪ   budɛʃ   miːt   ʒɛnɔ   kɔʒɛʃɪnu   jak   ɦrabjɛŋka]

a   ty   budeš   mít,   ženo,   kožešinu   jak   hraběnka.″
and   you   will   have,   wife,   fur   like   countess.″

and you will have, my wife, a fur like a countess.″

[nɛstɪd'iːʃ   sɛ   d'ɛdɔ   zviːr̝ɛ   tɛːrat]

[46]Nestydíš se,   dědo,   zvíře   térat?
Aren't you ashamed,   old man,   animal   to torture?

Aren't you ashamed, old man, to torture an animal?

(Lišák se staví čím dál tím víc do postoje, pln údivu.)
(The fox looks on with increasing intensity, full of astonishment.)

[ʔɛslɪ ʔudɛriːʃ znɔva pɔstaviːm sɛ   tʼɪ]

Esli uderíš znova postavím se   ti!
If you hit   again I'll take a stand against you!

If you hit me again I'll attack you!

[t͡sɔ   sɛʃ tak lakɔmɛː]

Co   seš tak lakomé,
Why   are you so stingy

Why are you so stingy

[ʒɛ   ⁱdɛ   tʼɪ   ʔɔ ‿ kɔːsɛk   ʒvant͡sa]

že   jde   ti   o   kósek   žvanca?
that it goes to you about little piece of morsel?

that you care about a piece of table scraps?

[maːʃ   tu   fʃɛfiɔ   dɔst ʔa jaː ɲɪt͡ʃɛfiɔʃ ɲɪt͡s]

Máš   tu   všeho   dost a já ničehož nic.
You have here of everything enough and I   at all   nothing.

You have here enough of everything, and I nothing at all.

[ʒɛbrat nɛːsu zvɪklaː tɔʃ sɛm sɪ kɔːsɛk vzala]

Žebrat nésu zvyklá, tož sem si kósek vzala.
To beg I'm not accustomed, so I - - small piece took.

I'm not used to begging, so I took a little bit.

[x͡tseʃ   ʔudɛr   x͡tseʃ   ʔudɛr]

Chceš,   uder!   Chceš,   uder!
You want,   hit!   You want,   hit!

If you want to, hit me! If you want to, hit me!

[pak   ʔajɪ   tɪ   ʔa   ʔudɛrɪl]

Pak   aji   ty—A   uderil!
Then   even   you—and   he struck!

Then even you—and he hit me!

(skřekem) (shrieking)
[tɪranɛ   tu   maːʃ   t͡sɔs x͡tsɛl]

Tyrane!   Tu   máš,   cos chcel!
Tyrant!   You   have,   what you wanted!

Tyrant! Now you get what you asked for!

[ʔa   zakɔliːbal   sɛ   jak   pɔtt'ateː strɔm   zdr̩fila   ⁱsɛm]

A   zakolíbal   se   jak   podt'até strom. Zdrhla   jsem.
And   he swayed   like   felled   tree.   I got the hell out.

And he swayed like a felled tree. I got the hell out of there.

[ʔa   s ‿ t'ɛɣ   dɔp   ⁱsɛm   zviːřɛ]

A   z   těch   dob   jsem   zvíře.
And   from those times   I am   animal.

And since then I've been an animal.

[lɛz   bɪl   t͡ʃɛrɲeⁱʃiː nɛʃ sama nɔt͡s ʔa   mɲɛ bɪlɔ vɔlnɔ]

Les byl černější než sama noc a mně bylo volno!
Forest was darker than itself night and to me it was free!

The forest was darker than night itself, and I felt free!

Lišák:

(Pokloní se hluboko Bystroušce.) (He bows deeply to Bystrouška.)
(Pln údivu se představuje) (Filled with wonder he introduces himself.)

[zlatɔfɪřbiːtɛk   lɪʃaːk   s ‿ krɔuʃkɔviːmɪ   pɛsiːkɪ]

Zlatohřbítek, lišák s kroužkovými pesíky,
Goldenback,   fox   with   curly   fur,

"Goldenback," the fox with curly fur,

[z ‿ filubɔkɛː   zmɔlɪ]

z Hluboké zmoly.
from Deep ravine.

from Deep Ravine.

Bystrouška:

[t'ɛʃiː   mnɛ   bɪstrɔuʃka]

Těší mne! Bystrouška,
It pleases me!   Sharpie,

Pleased to meet you! "Sharpie,"

(podává mu pravou tlapku) (offers him her right paw)
[sxɔvaŋka   z ⌣ jɛzɛrskɛ: mɪslɪvnɪ]

schovanka   z   Jezerské   myslivny.
foster cub   from   Lake   forester's lodge.

foster cub from Forester's Lodge on the Lake.

Lišák:

(políbí Bystroušce koneček tlapky)
(he kisses the tip of Bystrouška's paw)

[47]see note

(rozechvěně) (excitedly)
[nɛbudɛ   va:m   slɛt͡ʃnɔ   nɛmɪlɛ:]

Nebude   vám,   slečno,   nemilé,
It will not be   to you,   miss,   unpleasant,

It won't be unpleasant for you, miss,

[gdɪbɪx   va:s   ʔɔpjɛt   nafʃt'i:vɪl]

kdybych   vás   opět   navštívil?
if I were to   you   again   call on?

if I were to call on you again?

Bystrouška: (upejpavě) (coyly, shyly)

[dɔzajɪsta   ɲɪkɔlɪ]

[48]**Dozajista   nikoli.**
Certainly   not at all.

Certainly not at all.

Lišák:

[xɔd'iːvaːtɛ   t͡ʃastɔ   na ‿ palɔut͡ʃɛk]

Chodíváte   často   na   palouček?
Do you come   often   to   small glade?

Do you come often to the small glade?

[49]**Bystrouška:**

[mɛzɪ   puːlnɔt͡siː   ʔa   jɛdnɔu]

Mezi   půlnocí   a   jednou.
Between   midnight   and   one.

Between midnight and one.

[nɛmaːm   pR̝iːtɛlɛ   tɔʃ   xɔd'iːm   sama]

Nemám   přítele,   tož   chodím   sama.
I don't have   friend,   so   I walk   alone.

I don't have a friend, so I walk alone.

[ɲɪkɔmu   nɛdɔvɔliːm   ʔabɪ   mnɛ   dɔprɔvaːzɛl]

Nikomu   nedovolím,   aby   mne   [50]doprovázel!
To no one   do I permit,   that he   me   would accompany!

I don't permit anyone to accompany me!

Lišák:

[ˈɪstɛ   ʔɪdɛaːl   mɔdɛrɲiː   ʒɛnɪ   kɔuřiːtɛ   snat]

Jste   [51]ideál   moderní   ženy!   Kouříte   snad?
You are   ideal   modern   of woman! Do you smoke perhaps?

You are the ideal modern woman!   Do you smoke perhaps?

Bystrouška: Lišák:

[jɛʃt'ɛ   nɛʔɛ]   [ʒɛrɛtɛ   kraːliːkɪ]

Ještě   nee.   **Žerete   králíky?**
Still   no.   Do you eat   rabbits?

Not yet.   *Do you eat rabbits?*

Bystrouška: Lišák:
                              (odporučuje se) (he takes his leave)
[ʔɔː   jak   raːda]   [ruku   liːbaːm]

Ó,   jak   ráda!   **[52]Ruku   líbám!**
Oh,   how   with pleasure!   Hand   I kiss!

Oh, I love it!   *Au revoir!*

                              (Odkvapí.) (He hurries off.)

Bystrouška: (ulehne na hřbet, natáhne prut)
(she lies on her back, she spreads out her tail)

[ˈsɛmlɪ   ʔɔpravdu   tak | krraːsnaː]

Jsem-li   opravdu   tak   krásná?
Am I if   really   so   beautiful?

Am I really so beautiful?

(Válí se v písku.) (She rolls in the sand.)

(Čistí se.) (She cleans herself.)

[t͡sɔ   jɛ   na ‿ mɲɛ   tak | kraːsnɛːɦɔ]

[53]Co je   na   mně   tak   krásného?
What is   about   me   so   beautiful?

What is so beautiful about me?

(Uléhá si opět.) (She lies down again.)

(Hladí se, srovnává si pesíky.)
(She strokes herself, she tidies up her fur.)

[t͡sɔ   jɛ   na ‿ mɲɛ   tak | krraːsnɛːɦɔ]

Co je   na   mně   tak   krásného?
What is   about   me   so   beautiful?

What is so beautiful about me?

(Lišák vrací se; schován za křovím potutelně Bystroušku pozoruje.)
(Lišák returns; hidden behind bushes, surreptitiously he observes Bystrouška.)

[t͡sɔ   jɛ   na ‿ mɲɛ   tak | kraːsnɛːɦɔ]

Co je   na   mně   tak   krásného?
What is   about me   so   beautiful?

What is so beautiful about me?

[trɔxu   ⁱsɛm   pR̝et͡sɛ   k ‿ svjɛtu]

Trochu   jsem   přece   ⁵⁴k   světu!
A little   I am   after all   to   world!

I am quite pretty, though!

[tɪ   d'ɪvnɛː   ʔa   t͡ʃarɔkrraːsnɛː   mɪʃlɛŋkɪ]

Ty   divné   a   čarokrásné   myšlenky!
These   strange and   magically beautiful   thoughts!

These strange and magical beautiful thoughts!

Lišák: (k sobě) (to himself)

[ɦɛzɔuŋkaː jɛ   ɦɛzɔuŋkaː nɛsmiːm sɪ jɪ nɛxat pR̝ɛbrat]

Hezounká je,   hezounká! Nesmím si ji nechat přebrat!
Pretty one she is, pretty one! I may not – her let entice away!

*She is pretty, pretty! I must not let anyone entice her away
from me!*

Bystrouška:

(k sobě) (to herself)
[ˈsɛmlɪ ʔɔpravdu   tak | kraːsnaː   muːⁱ   sɪnɛt͡ʃku   zlatiː]

Jsem-li   opravdu   tak   krásná?   Můj   synečku   zlatý!
Am I-if   really   so   beautiful?   My   lover   gold!

Am I really so beautiful? My gold darling!

Lišák: (nesměle vystoupí) (shyly he comes out)

[ruku   liːbaːm]

Ruku   líbám.
Hand   I kiss.

Greetings.

Bystrouška:

[gdɪbɪs   vjɛdʼɛl jak   ⁱsɛm   sɛ   dɔ‿ tɛbɛ   zamɪlɔvala]

Kdybys   věděl,   jak   jsem   se   do [55]tebe   zamilovala?
Would you know   how   I have   -   with   you   fallen in love?

Would you know how I have fallen in love with you?

(Lekem vyskočí.) (She jumps to her feet.)

Lišák:	Bystrouška:

[ruku   liːbaːm]   [t͡sɔ   vɪ   pR̝ɪxaːziːtɛ tak   t͡ʃasɲɛ]

Ruku	**líbám.**	**Co**	**vy**	**přicházíte**	**tak**	**časně?**
Hand	I kiss.	What	you	arrive	so	early?

Greetings.   *Why do you come so soon?*

(Ukazuje Bystroušce králíka.) (He shows Bystrouška the rabbit.)

Lišák:	Bystrouška:

[xɪ   xɪ   xɪ]   [xɪ   xɪ   xɪ   xɪ]

[56]**Chi chi chi!**   **Chi chi chi chi!**

Ha ha ha!   *Ha ha ha ha!*

Lišák:

[xɪ   xɪ   xɪ   tadɪ   vaːm   nɛsu   ɲɛt͡sɔ   k‿sɲɛtku]

Chi chi chi! Tady   vám   nesu   něco   k snědku!
                Here   to you I bring something to eat!

Ha ha ha! Here I bring you something to eat!

[xɪ   xɪ   xɪ]

Chi   chi   chi!

Ha ha ha!

Bystrouška:

(klade před Bystroušku mladého králíka)
(he lays the young rabbit in front of Bystrouška)

[xɪ xɪ xɪ xɪ　　　　vɪ　ⁱstɛ　ʔɔʃklɪvɛː]

Chi chi chi chi!　　**Vy　jste　ošklivé—**
　　　　　　　　　　　　You　are　naughty

Ha ha ha ha!　　*You're naughty—*

[dʼɛlaːtɛ sɪ　kvuːlɪvaː　mɲɛ　takɔvɔu　ʃkɔdu]

děláte　si　kvůlivá　mně　takovou　škodu.
　you make　because of　me　such　expenditure.

you make such a fuss because of me.

Lišák:

[xɪ　xɪ　xɪ]

Chi chi chi!

Ha ha ha!

(Pokroutí si junácky vous, zahledí se zamilovně.)
(He twists his moustache robustly, he gazes lovingly.)

(Usedají k posnídávce.) (They sit down to breakfast.)

[jɛ　vaːm　zɪma]

Je　vám　zima?
Is it　to you　cold?

Are you cold?

Bystrouška: (šeptá) (she whispers)

[nɛʔɛ   jɛ   mɪ   fiɔrkɔ]

Nee, je   mi   horko!
No,   it is to me   hot!

No, I'm hot!

(Ranní červánky) (Morning red sky)

(Lišák skloní hlavu, složí prut souměrně s Bystrouščiným a vtiskne Bystroušce první pocel na ouško.)
(Lišák bows his head, lays his tail parallel with Bystrouška's, and places his first kiss on her ear.)

Lišák:

[vɪ   ⁱstɛ   jɛʃt'ɛ   nɛmɪlɔvala]

Vy   jste   ještě   nemilovala?
You   did   yet   not love?

Were you ever in love?

Bystrouška: (stydlivě) (shyly)	Lišák:	Bystrouška:
[nɛʔɛ ʔa vɪ mɔts͡]	[takɪ nɛʔɛ]	[prɔt͡ʃ]
Nee! A vy moc?	**Taky nee.**	**Proč?**
No! And you a lot?	Also no.	Why?
No! And you a lot?	*Also no.*	*Why?*

Lišák:

[prɔtɔ   ʒɛ   ⁱsɛm   jɛʃt'ɛ   nɛnaʃɛl   takɔvɛː]

Proto,   **že**   **jsem**   **ještě**   **nenašel**   **takové,**
Because,   that   I did   still   not find   such,

Because, I still didn't find anyone

[kɛrɛː   bɪx   sɪ   jaː   bɪl   vaːʒɪl]

keré   **bych**   **si**   **já**   **byl**   **vážil,**
whom   I would   -   I   have   respected,

whom I would have respected,

[prɔ‿ kterɔu   bɪɣ   ʒɪvɔt   dal   ʔalɛ naⁱdulɪ takɔvɛː]

pro   **kterou**   **bych**   **život**   **dal.**   **Ale**   **najdu-li takové,**
for   whom   I would   life   give.   But   I find-if   such,

for whom I would give my life. But if I find such a one,

Bystrouška: Lišák:

(hrdlo se jí sevře)
(her throat closes up)

[tɔʃ]   [tɔʒ bɛz‿vɛlkɛːɦɔ rɔzmɪʃlɛɲiː zɛptaːm sɛ jiː]

tož . . .   **tož bez**   **velkého rozmyšlení zeptám se jí:**
then . . .   then without big   reflection   I will ask her:

then . . .   *then without thinking twice I'll ask her:*

Bystrouška:

[tɔʃ]

tož . . .
then . . .

then . . .

Lišák:

(Bystrouška blízka mdlobě)   (obejme Bystroušku)
(Bystrouška close to fainting)   (embraces Bystrouška)

[maːʃlɪ   mnɛ   raːda   vɪ   ml̩t͡ʃiːtɛ]

Máš-li   mne   [57]ráda?   Vy   mlčíte?
You have-if   me   love?   You   are silent?

"Do you love me?"   You're silent?

(Lišák zuřivě schvátí Bystroušku.)
(Lišák passionately seizes Bystrouška.)

Bystrouška:

[pustʼtɛ   mnɛ   butʼtɛ   tak   laskavɛː]

Pusťte   mne!   Buďte   tak   laskavé!
Let go   me!   Be   so   kind!

Let go of me! Be so kind!

[stɛ   firɔznɛː   bɔjiːm sɛ   vaːs]

Ste   **hrozné!**   **Bojím se**   **vás!**
You are   horrible!   I'm afraid of   you!

You're horrible! I'm afraid of you!

[d'ɪtɛ   prɪt͡ʃ   nɛxt͡su   vaːs   vɪd'ɛt]

Dite   **pryč!**   **Nechcu**   **vás**   **vidět!**
Go   away!   I don't want   you   to see!

Go away! I don't want to see you!

(Pustí ji smutně.) (He sadly lets her go.)

Lišák:

[tɔʃ   tɔʒ   bjɛʃtɛ   ʔɔdnɛstɛ mɔjɛ   ʃt'ɛst'iː   zɲɪt͡ʃtɛ   mnɛ]

Tož,   **tož běžte, odneste moje**   **štěstí!**   **Zničte**   **mne!**
Then,   then run,   take away my   happiness!   Destroy   me!

Then, then run away, take away my happiness! Destroy me!

[skastɛ   mnɛ   nɛxt͡su   bɪt   ʒɪveː]

Zkazte   **mne!**   **Nechcu**   **byt**   **živé!**
Ruin   me!   I don't want   to be   alive!

Ruin me! I don't want to be alive!

Bystrouška:

[ʔɔpravdu   prɔt͡ʃ   stɛ   tɔ   neřɛkḷ   dři:vɛ]

Opravdu?   Proč   ste   to   neřekl   dříve?
Really?   Why   did you   it   not say   earlier?

Really? Why didn't you say so earlier?

(Utírá si čumáček.)
(She wipes her muzzle.)

Lišák:

[ʔɔpravdu   tɛbɛ   bɪstrɔuʃkɔ   ⁱsɛm   sɪ ja: zamɪlɔval]

Opravdu, ⁵⁸tebe, Bystrouško, jsem si já   zamiloval.
Really,   you, Bystrouška, have -   I   fallen in love with.

Really, it's you, Bystrouška, I fell in love with.

Bystrouška:

[mnɛ   mnɛ]

Mne!   Mne!
Me!   Me!

Me! Me!

Lišák: (vášnivě) (passionately)

[ʔɔpravdu tɛbɛ   tɛbɛ   bɪstrɔuʃkɔ   tɛbɛ   bɪstrɔuʃkɔ]

Opravdu tebe, tebe, Bystrouško, tebe, Bystrouško,
Really   you, you, Bystrouška, you, Bystrouška,

Really you, you, Bystrouška, you, Bystrouška,

[tɛbɛ   ⁱsɛm   sɪ   zamɪlɔval]

tebe   jsem   si   zamiloval,
you   did I   fall in love with,

you I fell in love with,

[prɔtɔʒɛ ⁱsɪ   zrɔvna takɔvaː jakɔu ⁱsɛm ʔɔdjagʒɪva x͡tsɛl]

protože jsi zrovna taková, jakou jsem ⁵⁹odjakživa chcel!
because you're just   such,   like I have always wanted!

because you're just what I have always wanted!

Bystrouška:

[prɔd͡ʒ   zrɔvna   mnɛ prɔd͡ʒ   zrɔvna   mnɛ]

Proč   zrovna   ⁶⁰mne? Proč   zrovna   ⁶⁰mne?
Why   exactly   me?   Why   exactly   me?

Why exactly me? Why exactly me?

Lišák:

[nɛⁱsu   lɦaːř̩   nɛⁱsu   lɪʃaːk   ʔulfianɛː]

Nejsu   lhář,   nejsu   lišák   ulhané.
I'm not   liar,   I'm not   fox   lying.

I'm not a liar, I'm not a lying fox.

[mluviːm   t͡sɔ   f ‿ sr̩t͡sɪ   nɔsiːm   ʔɔt ‿ ft͡ʃiːrka]

Mluvím,   co   v   srdci   nosím   od   ⁶¹včírka.
I speak   what   in   heart   I carry   since   yesterday.

I speak what I carry in my heart since yesterday.

[nɛ   t'ɛlɔ   tvɔju   duʃu   mɪluju   nɛvr̩d͡z   fɪlavɔu]

Ne   tělo,   tvoju   dušu   miluju.   Nevrc   hlavou.
Not   body,   your   soul   I love.   Don't shake   head.

It's not your body, it's your soul I love. Don't shake your head.

[ʔuvɪd'iːʃ   bɪstrɔuʃkɔ   mɔja   ʔuvɪd'iːʃ   ʒɛ   ʔaⁱ   rɔmaːnɪ]

Uvidíš,   Bystrouško moja, uvidíš,   že aj romány,
You will see, Bystrouška   my, you will see, that even novels,

You will see, my Bystrouška, you will see that even novels

[ʔɔpɛrɪ budɔu ʔɔ‿ tɔbjɛ psaːt'ɪ pɔⁱt' sɛm   nɛut'iːkɛː]

opery budou o   tobě [62]**psáti. Pojd̆ sem,** [63]**neutíké.**
operas they'll about you   write. Come here, don't run away.

and operas will be written about you. Come here, don't run
away.

[sɛdɲɪ   sɪ   vɛdlɪvaː   mnɛ]

Sedni   si   vedlivá   mne.
Sit   yourself next to   me.

Sit next to me.

(Schvátí Bystroušku a líbá ji vášnivě.)
(He embraces Bystrouška and kisses her passionately.)

[xt͡sɛʃ   mɪ   nɛplat͡ʃ]

Chceš   mi?   Neplač!
Do you want   me?   Don't cry!

Do you want me? Don't cry!

[ʔajɪ   jaː   bɪx   rradɔst'ɔu   zaplakal]

[64]**Aji   já   bych   radost̆ ou   zaplakal!**
Even   I   would   from joy   cry!

Even I would cry from joy!

[xt͡sɛʃ   mɪ   xt͡sɛʃ   mɪ]

Chceš   **mi?**   **⁶⁵Chceš**   **mi?**
Do you want   me?   Do you want   me?

Do you want me? Do you want me?

Bystrouška: (pokorně) (humbly)

[xt͡su]

Chcu!   (Vklouzne s Lišákem do doupěte.)
I want!   (She slips into the lair with the Fox.)

I do! I do!

[xt͡su]

Chcu!
I want!

I do!

Modrá vážka   Blue dragonfly
(baletní výkon)   (ballet performance)

(Sova přiletí jako stín; sojka za ní.)
(The Owl flies in like a shadow; the Jay is behind her.)

Sova: (křičí do lesa) (she screeches in the direction of the forest)

[gdɪbɪstɛ   vjɛd'ɛlɪ   t͡sɔ   jaː   vɪd'ɛla]

Kdybyste   **věděli,**   **co**   **já**   **viděla,**
If you were to know   what   I   saw,

If you only knew what I saw,

[t'ɛmatɔ   vlastɲiːma   ʔɔt͡ʃɪma   vɪd'ɛla   jaː   staraː   ʔɔsɔba]

těmato   vlastníma   očima   viděla,   já   stará   osoba!
with those   my own   eyes   saw,   I   old   person!

saw with my own eyes, at my age!

[ta   naʃa   bɪstrɔuʃka   jɛ   jak   ta   nɛⁱfiɔrʃiː]

Ta   naša   Bystrouška   je   jak   ta   nejhorší.
That   our   Bystrouška   is   like   that   worst.

That Bystrouška of ours is the worst.

Sojka:

[s ‿ kɛːm]

S   kém?
With   whom?

With whom?   Slunce vychází. The sun rises.

(Veverky se chichlají; ježek za pařezem vyplazuje jazyk.)
(The squirrels giggle: a hedgehog behind a tree stump sticks out his tongue.)

Bystrouška: (vzlyká, vylézá z doupěte) (she sobs, she crawls out of her lair)

[ʔaɔɔu   ʔaɔɔu   ʔaɔɔu]

Aoou!   Aoou!   Aoou!
Ow!   Ow!   Ow!

Ow! Ow! Ow!

Lišák: (vylézá z doupěte) (he crawls out from her lair)

[t͡sɔ   plaːt͡ʃɛʃ   naři:ka:ʃ]

Co   pláčeš,   naříkáš?
Why   are you crying,   are you moaning?

Why are you crying and moaning?

[t͡sɔ   sɛ t'ɪ   stalɔ   duʃɛŋkɔ   ʒɛs   tak ʔuplakana:]

Co   se ti   stalo,   dušenko,   žes   tak uplakaná?
What - to you happened, dear soul, that you're so tearful?

What happened to you, darling, that you are so tearful?

Bystrouška:

[ʔa   tɪ   nɛvi:ʃ   t͡sɔ   tɪ   nɛtuʃi:ʃ]

A   ty   nevíš,   co   ty   netušíš?
And   you   don't know why   you   don't guess?

And you don't know, why don't you guess?

Lišák:

[nɛʔɛ   pɔvjɛs   mɪ   tɔ]

⁶⁶Nee,   pověz   mi   to.
No,   tell   to me it.

No, tell me.

(Šeptá mu do ucha.) (She whispers in his ear.)

(Padne mu okolo krku.) (She drops to his neck.)

(Sklesnou mu přední tlapky, vzdychne si.)
(His front paws droop, he sighs.)

[gdɪʃ   jɛ   tɔ   tak]

Když   je   to   tak,
If   is   it   so,

If it's so,

Bystrouška:

[t͡sɔ   ft͡ʃɪl   mɪsliːʃ   sɛ ‿ mnɔu   dʼɛlat]

Co   včil   myslíš   se   mnou   dělat?
What   now   do you think   with   me   to do?

What are you thinking of doing with me now?

Lišák:

[tɔʃ   rɔvnɔu   k ‿   faraːřɔvɪ]

tož   rovnou   k   farářovi!
then   straight   to   pastor!

then straight to the pastor!

(Datel vystrčí hlavu ze starého jeřábu.)
(The Woodpecker pokes his head out from an old mountain-ash tree.)

Datel:

(nevrlé) (irritably)

[nɔ   ʒɛ   ʔuʃ   dɛtɛ]

No,   **že   už   dete!**
Well,   that already   you come!

Well, finally you come!

[t͡ʃɛɦɔ   sɪ   vlastɲɛ   pR̝ɛjɛtɛ]

⁶⁷**Čeho si   vlastně   přejete?**
What   -   actually   do you desire?

What do you want, then?

Hlas lesa: (Za scénou)   (Behind the scene)

[ʔɔː]

⁶⁸**Ó**

Oh!

Lišák:

[mɪ   bɪxɔm   tɛntɔnɔnt͡s   raːdʼɪ   svadbu]

My   bychom,   tentononc,   rádi   svatbu!
We would,   uh,   like wedding!

We would, uh, like a wedding!

Datel:

[spiːʃ   ʔɔfilaːʃkɪ   nɛ]

Spíš   ohlášky?   Ne?
Rather banns?   No?

You mean marriage banns? No?

(Oddává je.) (He marries them.)

[tɛntɔnɔn͡ts   lɪʃaːk   zlatɔfɪ̌rbiːtɛk   bɛrɛ   sɪ]

[69]**Tentononc Lišák   Zlatohřbítek   bere si**
    Uh,   fox   Goldenback   takes

Uh, the fox "Goldenback" takes

[lɪʃku   bɪstrɔuʃku   za ‿ manʒɛlku]

lišku   Bystroušku   za   manželku.
vixen   Sharpie   for   wife.

the vixen "Sharpie" for his wife.

(Svatební rej) (Wedding dance)
(Baletní výkon) (Ballet performance)

[70]see note

Opona Curtain

Konec II. jednání   End of Act II

Act III

III. Jednání
Act III [Scene i]

Opona Curtain

Na kraji seče (Podzim, poledne, jasná obloha)
At the edge of the clearing (Autumn, noon, clear sky)

Harašta (s prázdnou putnou na zádech, jde cestičkou do vrchu)
Harašta (with an empty basket on his back, he walks uphill)

Revírník (s puskou na rameni jde cestičkou s vrchu)
Forester (with his rifle on his shoulder he walks downhill)

[The following stage direction occurs in the orchestral score, but not in the piano/vocal score, at reh. 4, for Harašta as he enters the scene:

Prozpěvuje si   He sings merrily]

(Rev. zhlédne zdaleka Haraštu.)
(The Forester watches Harašta from a distance)

Harašta: ¹see note

[dɛːʃ sɛm vandrɔval   mɔzɛka firaːla mɔja   znɛːmɪlɛːʃiː]

Déž   sem   vandroval, mozeka hrála, moja   znémiléší,
When   I wandered,   music   played, my   dearest,

When I went wandering, the music was playing, my dearest,

[mɔja   znɛːmɪlɛːʃiː   s ‿ ʔɔkna   kɔːkalalalala]

moja   znémíléší   z   okna   kókalalalala,
my   dearest   from window   she g-g-gazed,

my dearest g-g-g-gazed from the window,

[s ‿ ʔɔkna   kɔːkala]

z   okna   kókala.
from window   she gazed.

she gazed from the window.

[nɛkɔːkɛː   za ‿ mnɔː]

Nekóké   za   mnó,
Don't look   at   me,

Don't look at me,

[pɔt'   rɛːʃɪ   sɛ ‿ mnɔː ʔa   jaː   tɔbjɛ   kɔːpiːm]

pod'   réši   se   mnó   a   já   tobě   kópím,
come   better with   me   and I   you   will buy,

better come with me and I'll buy you,

[ʔa   jaː   tɔbjɛ   kɔːpiːm   sɔkɲɔ   zɛlɛnɔːnɔːnɔːnɔː   sɔkɲɔ   zɛlɛnɔː]

a   já   tobě   kópím   sokňo   zelenónónónó,   sokňo   zelenó.
and I   you   will buy skirt   gr-gr-gr-green,   skirt   green.

and I'll buy you a gr-gr-gr-green skirt, a green skirt.

[sɔkɲɔ   zɛlɛnɔː mɛzɔlanɔvɔː ɦabɛ tɛ sɛ mɔfila]

Sokňo   zelenó   mezolanovó,   habe te se mohla,
Skirt   green   woolen,   so that you could,

A green woolen skirt, so that you could,

[ɦabɛ tɛ sɛ mɔfila vandrɔvat   sɛ ‿ mnɔːnɔːnɔːnɔː]

habe te se mohla vandrovat se   mnónónónó,
so that you could   wander   with m-m-m-me,

so that you could wander with m-m-m-me,

[vandrɔvat   sɛ ‿ mnɔː]

vandrovat   se   mnó.
wander   with me.

wander with me.

(Zhlédne nataženého zajíce; chce ho vzít, ale tu uvidí myslivce.)
(He sees a dead hare; he wants to pick it up, but then he sees the gamekeeper.)

Revírník: (zhurta) (brusquely)

[tɔʃ   t͡sɔ   ɦaraʃtɔ   maːʃ   sɛ   dɔbr̝ɛ]

²Tož   co,   Harašto,   máš   se   dobře?
Then   what,   Harašta,   you have   yourself   well?

So, Harašta, are you doing well?

Harašta:

[nu t͡sɔʃ   pantaːtɔ mɲɛl bɪx sɛ   dɔbr̝ɛ]

Nu, což	**pantáto,**	**měl**	**bych se**	**dobře,**
Well,	neighbor,	I would be		well,

Well, neighbor, I would be well

[gdɪ bɪ   nɛ tɛː mɔjɪ   suːʒɛ]

kdy	**by**	**ne**	**té**	**moji**	**súže!**
if they were		not	these	my	troubles!

if I didn't have any worries!

Revírník:

[mɪsliːm sɪ   jak   sɛ ʔɔbɛndɛʃ bɛz ‿ ʒɛnɪ]

Myslím si,	**jak**	**se obendeš**	**bez**	**ženy?**
I mean,	how	do you manage	without	wife?

I mean, how do you manage without a wife?

Harašta:

[zaʔɔbɛndu sɛ   pjɛkɲɛ zaʔɔbɛndu]

Zaobendu se,	**pěkně**	**zaobendu.**
I manage,	nicely	I manage.

I manage, I manage nicely.

[ʔalɛ ft͡ʃɪl zlataː tɪ mɔja rɛpublɪkɔ]

Ale   včil,   zlatá   ty   moja   republiko,
But   now,   golden you   my   republic,

But now, by golly,

[daːm sɛ   s ‿ ɲɔu zɛzdat]

dám   se   s   ňou   zezdat!
I give myself with   her   to marry!

I'm going to marry her!

[daːm sɛ   s‿ ɲɔu zɛzdat]

Dám   se   s   ňou   zezdat!
I give myself with   her   to marry!

I'm going to marry her!

[fʃak   pantaːtɔ naʃɛl ᶦsɛm   sɪ   tu   neːlɛpt͡ʃiː]

Však,   pantáto, našel jsem   si   tu   nélepčí.
Because,   neighbor, I found   myself that   best.

Because, neighbor, I've found the best woman.

[tɔtɔk]

Totok,   (vytahuje láhev z kapsy) (he pulls a bottle from his pocket)
This,

This,

[tɔtɔk   jiː   nɛsu   na ‿ zvɔstŘɛnɔː]

totok   jí   nesu   na   zvostřenó!
this   to her   I'm taking to   focus/give spice to/liven up!

I'm taking this to her to put her in the mood!

(Zatřepe lahvičkou, pohledne na bublinky a upije statečně.)
(He shakes the bottle, looks at the bubbles, and gulps down a lot.)

(důvěrně) (confidentially)
[jɛ   jiː   tɛrɪŋka]

Je   jí   Terynka!
She is   with her   Terynka!

She's Terynka!

Revírník: Harašta:

[tɛrɪŋka]   [baʒɛ   tɛrɪŋka]

Terynka?   **Baže,   Terynka!**
Terynka?   Sure,   Terynka!

Terynka?   *Sure, Terynka!*

Revírník: (nedůvěřivě) (in disbelief))   Harašta: (radostně)
                                                       (joyfully)
[tɛrɪŋka]   [tɛrɪŋka   tɛrɪŋka]

Terynka?   **Terynka, Terynka!**

Terynka?   *Terynka, Terynka!*

Revírník: (přísně) (sternly)

[ʔa   nɛpɪtlat͡ʃiːʃ   mɪ   ɦaraʃtɔ]

A   nepytlačíš   mi,   Harašto?
And   you're not poaching   to me,   Harašta?

And you're not poaching, are you, Harašta?

Harašta: (s přetvářkou) (with hypocrisy)

[jak   jɛ   buːx   nɛdɛ   mnɔː]

Jak   je   Bůh   nede   mnó
As   is   God   above   me

As God is above me

[ʔa   tvr̩daː   zɛm   pɔdɛ   mnɔː   ʔaɲɪ   ʔaɲɪ   brɔkɛm]

a   tvrdá   zem   pode   mnó,   ani,   ani   brokem!
and   hard   earth   under me,   not,   not   grain of shot!

and the hard earth is under me, not a single shot!

[ʔalɛ   ʔalɛ   skɔrɔ   mɲɛl   bɪx]

Ale,   ale   skoro   měl   bych!
But,   but   almost   I should!

But, but, maybe I should! '

Revírník:

[t͡sɔ   tɔ   plɛndaːʃ]

Co   **to**   **plendáš?!**
What   it   you're babbling?!

What's that you're babbling?!

Harašta: (tajemně) (secretively)

[nɔ   tɔʃ   tu   paːr krɔkuː lɛʒiː zajiːt͡s ʔa   nataʒɛnɛː]

No, [3]tož,   **tu**   **pár kroků leží**   **zajíc!**   **A**   **natažené!**
Well,   there   few   steps   lies   hare!   And   dead!

Well, there's a hare a few steps away! And it's dead!

[xtʼɛl   ⁱsɛm   ɦɔ   vziːt   ʔalɛ   ʔɛʃt͡ʃɛ   ʒɛ   mɪ]

Chtěl   **jsem**   **ho**   **vzít,**   **ale**   **ešče**   **že**   **mi,**
I wanted   him   to take,   but   still   that   to me,

I wanted to take it, but then,

[ʒɛ   mɪ   t͡sɔsɪ   řɛklɔ]

že   **mi**   **cosi**   **řeklo:**
that   to me   something   said:

but then something said to me:

[nɛbɛr   fiaraʃtɔ   mɔfiḷ   bɪs   biːt   f‿ ʔɔstud'ɛ]

Neber,   Harašto,   mohl bys   být   v   ⁴ostudě!
Don't take,   Harašta,   you could   be   in   disgrace!

"Don't take it, Harašta, you could be discredited!"

Revírník:

[t͡ʃlɔvjɛt͡ʃɛ]

Člověče!
Man!

Man!

(Div ho nosem neprobodne.)
(It's a wonder he doesn't poke him with his nose.)

[sɛtsakrapɛs]

Setsakrapes!

Good heavens!

[nɛbɛr   fiaraʃtɔ nɛbɛr   mɔfiḷ bɪs   biːt   f‿ ʔɔstud'ɛ]

Neber,   Harašto, neber,   mohl bys být v   ostudě!
Don't take,   Harašta, don't take,   you could   be   in   disgrace!

Don't take it, Harašta, you could be discredited!

(Přehodí pušku a jde rovnou k seči.)
(He slings the gun on his shoulder and walks straight toward the clearing.)

[In the orchestra: (naříkavě) (plaintively)]

(Harašta vychytrale za ním.) (Harašta slyly behind him.)

[ʔa nataʒɛnɛː]

A   natažené?
And   dead?

And it's dead?

Harašta: (nadsázkou) (exaggerating)

[ʔa natazɛnɛː]

A   natažené!
And   dead!

And it's dead!

(Na kraji seče leží zajíc studený; u něho liščí stopy.)
(At the edge of the clearing lies a cold hare; around it, a vixen's foot-prints.)

Revírník:

[ʒɛ   ʔuʃ   pɔkɔjɛ   nɛdaː]

Že   už   pokoje   nedá!
That   already peace   she doesn't give!

When will she give me some peace!

(Vytahuje železa z vaku.) (He pulls a trap out of his bag.)

(Nalíkne železa.) (He sets the trap.)

[lɪʃka   bɪstrɔuʃka   naliːknɛm]

Liška   Bystrouška!   Nalíknem.
Vixen   Bystrouška!   We'll set a trap.

The vixen Bystrouška! We'll set a trap.

[bɛstak   prɔ‿ maʈska   sɛ vraːtʼiː]

Beztak   pro ⁵macka   se vrátí.
Anyway   for   plump hare   she'll return.

Anyway, she'll return for the hare.

(Zamračen zabočí do žlebu.) (Frowning, he turns toward the ravine.)

(Harašta dívá se vychytrale za revírníkem.)
(Harašta looks slyly behind the Forester.)

Harašta: (potutelně) (secretively)

[XI   XI   XI   XI   XI   XI]

Chi chi chi! Chi chi chi!
Ha ha ha! Ha ha ha!

(Odchází opačným směrem.)
(He walks away in the opposite direction.)

[XI   XI   XI]

Chi chi chi!

Ha ha ha!

Vyběhnou lištičky   The Fox Cubs run out
(Baletní výkon) (Ballet performance)

Lištičky:

[6]see note

[bjeʒiː lɪʃka k ‿ taːbɔru   nɛsɛ   pɪtɛl   zaːzvɔru]

Běží   liška   k   [7]Táboru,   nese   pytel   [8]zázvoru,
Runs   vixen   to   Tábor,   she carries   sack   of ginger,

A vixen is running to Tábor, carrying a sack of ginger,

[bjeʃ zajiːtʃku bjeʃ   za ‿ ɲiː   pɔbɛr   jiː   tɔ kɔřɛɲiː]

běž,   zajíčku,   běž   za   ní,   pober   jí   to   koření.
run,   hare,   run   after   her,   take all   from her those spices.

run, hare, run after her, take all the spices away from her.

[bjeʒiː lɪʃka k ‿ taːbɔru   nɛsɛ   pɪtɛl   bramboruː]

Běží   liška   k   Táboru,   nese   pytel   bramborů,
Runs   vixen   to   Tábor,   she carries   sack   of potatoes,

A vixen is running to Tábor, carrying a sack of potatoes,

[jeʒɛk   za ‿ ɲiː   pɔspiːxaː   ʒɛ   jiː   pɪtɛl   rɔspiːxaː]

ježek   za   ní   pospíchá,   že   jí   pytel   rozpíchá.
hedgehog   after her   hurries,   that   to her sack   he will rip up.

a hedgehog is hurrying after her to rip open her sack.

(Přiběhnou až k zajíci.) (They run up to the hare.)

Bystrouška:

[d'ɪvnaː vjet͡s d'ɪvnaː vjet͡s]

Divná věc!   Divná věc!   (Ohledává zajíce.)
Strange thing! Strange thing!   (She inspects the hare.)

How strange! How strange!

Lišák: Lištičky:

[d'ɪvnaː vjet͡s d'ɪvnaː vjet͡s]

Divná věc!   Divná věc!
Strange thing! Strange thing!

How strange! How strange!

Bystrouška:

[t͡ʃlɔvjɛk tu bɪl   ʔa zajiːt͡sɛ tu   zanɛxal]

Člověk   tu   byl, a   zajíce   tu   zanechal!
Man   here was, and hare   here he left!

A man was here, and he left the hare here!

Lišák: Lištičky:

[d'ɪvnaː vjet͡s d'ɪvnaː vjet͡s]

Divná věc!   Divná věc!
Strange thing! Strange thing!

How strange! How strange!

Bystrouška: Lišák: Laštičky:

[jɛ tɔ mɔʒnaː]   [d'ɪvnaː vjɛt͡s d'ɪvnaː vjɛt͡s]

Je   to   možná?   **Divná věc! Divná věc!**
Is   it   possible?   Strange thing! Strange thing!

Is it possible?   *How strange! How strange!*

Bystrouška:

[mɲɛl   fiɔ v ⏜ rut͡sɛ ʔa zasɛ fiɔ   pɔlɔʒɪl]

Měl   ho   v   ruce, a   zase   ho   položil.
He had it   in   hand, and again it   he put down.

He had it in his hands, and he put it down again.

Lišák:

[pɔzɔr   ʔuːklat]

Pozor!   Úklad!
Beware!   Plot!

Watch out! It's a trick!

Solo. 1. laštičky:

[ʔa jaː ʔuʃ viːm t͡sɔ tɔ jɛ   tɔ ⁱsɔu klɛʃt'ɛ]

A já už vím, co to je! To jsou kleště!
And I already know, what that is! Those are   trap clamps!

And I know what it is! It's a trap!

Bystrouška: (očenichává řetěz) (she sniffs at the chain)

[zatʃ͡   naːs   tɛn   d'ɛda   pɔvaʒujɛ]

Zač   nás   ten   děda   považuje?
For what us   that   old man considers?

What does that old man take us for?

Lištičky:

[tɔ   ᶦsɔu klɛʃt'ɛ   tɔ   ᶦsɔu klɛʃt'ɛ]

To   jsou kleště!   To   jsou kleště!
Those are   trap clamps! Those are   trap clamps!

It's a trap!   It's a trap!

[zatʃ͡   naːs   tɛn   d'ɛda   pɔvaʒujɛ]

Zač   nás   ten   děda   považuje?
For what us   that   old man considers?

What does that old man take us for?

Bystrouška:

[mɪsliː   ʒɛ   su   jɛzɛvet͡s]

Myslí,   že   su   jezevec?
Does he think that I am badger?

Does he take me for a badger?

Lištičky:

[mɪsliː   ʒɛ   su   jɛzɛveʦ]

Myslí,   že   su   jezevec?
Does he think   that   I am   badger?

Does he take me for a badger?

Bystrouška: Lišák: Lištičky:

[tɔ   ʔasɪ   nɛʔɛː]   [tɔ   ʔasɪ   nɛʔɛː]

To   asi   ⁹nee!   **To   asi   ⁹nee!**
That but   no!   That but   no!

Surely not!   *Surely not!*

Bystrouška:
                    (ušklíbne se) (she grins)
[jɛ   tɔ   ʔalɛ   jan   s ⌣ ʦedulɔu]

Je   to   ale   Jan   s   cedulou!
He is that   but   John   with   label!

He's a fool!

Lištičky:

[jan   s ⌣ ʦedulɔu jan   s ⌣ ʦedulɔu jan   s ⌣ ʦedulɔu]

Jan   s   cedulou! Jan   s   cedulou! Jan   s   cedulou!
John with   label!   John with   label!   John   with   label!

He's a fool! He's a fool! He's a fool!

Bystrouška:

[fajɛt͡ʃkɔu   smr̩d'iː   r̝ɛt'as]

Faječkou   smrdí   ¹⁰řet'az!
With pipe   stinks   chain!

The chain stinks of his pipe!

Lištičky:

[jan   s ‿ t͡sɛdulɔu   jan   s ‿ t͡sɛdulɔu]

Jan   s   cedulou!   Jan   s   cedulou!
John   with label!   John   with label!

He's a fool! He's a fool! He's a fool!

Bystrouška:

[mɪsliː   ʒɛ naːm nɛzvɔstal ʔaɲɪ jɛdɛn lɪʃt͡ʃiː   xlup]

Myslí,   že nám nezvostal ani jeden liščí   chlup?
Does he think that to us wasn't left even one of foxes' hair?

Does he think we don't have one single fox's hair left?

Lištičky: (rozběhnou se) (they run around)

[jan   s ‿ t͡sɛdulɔu]

Jan   s   cedulou!
John   with label!

He's a fool!

Lišák: (mazlí se s Bystr.) (he caresses Bystrouška)

[kɔlɪk   ⁱsmɛ   ʔuʃ   mɲɛlɪ   d'ɛt'iː]

Kolik   jsme   už   měli   dětí?
How many   did we already have children?

How many children have we had?

[staraː   nɛviːʃ]

Stará,   nevíš?
Old girl, don't you know?

Old girl, do you know?

Bystrouška:

[nɛviːm   kɔlɪk]

Nevím,   kolik.
I don't know   how many.

I don't know how many.

Lišák: (lísá se Bystr.) (he fawns on Bystrouška)

[ʔa   kɔlɪk   jɪx   jɛʃt'ɛ   budɛmɛ miːt'ɪ]

A   kolik   jich   ještě   budeme   míti?
And   how many   of them   still   will we   have?

And how many more of them will we have?

[staraː   nɛviːʃ]

Stará,   nevíš?
Old girl, don't you know?

Old girl, do you know?

Bystrouška:

[gdɪbɪs   dal pɔkɔja mɔfil̩ bɪ tʼɛ ɲɛgdɔ slɪʃɛt]

[11]**Kdybys   dal pokoja! Mohl by tě někdo slyšet.**
If you would give peace!   Could you someone hear.

Leave me in peace! Someone could hear you.

[znaːʃ   zviːr̝e͡tsiː   ɦubɪ]

Znáš   zvířecí   huby!
You know   animals'   muzzles!

You know how animals like to talk!

[dɔ‿ raːna   naːs rɔznɔsɪjɔː   pɔ‿   t͡sɛlɛːm lɛsu]

Do   rána   nás roznosijó   po   celém lesu.
To   morning us gossip about through whole forest.

By morning the whole forest will be gossiping about us.

Lišák:

[ʔa   t͡sɔʃ   kɔlɪk]

A   což   kolik?
And   well   how many?

Well, how many?

[jɛʃt'ɛ ⁱsɪ   nat͡ʃɪstɔ pjɛkna: jɛʃt'ɛ ⁱsɪ   nat͡ʃɪstɔ pjɛkna:]

Ještě   jsi   načisto pěkná, ještě   jsi   načisto pěkná!
Still   you are quite   pretty, still you are quite   pretty!

You're still quite beautiful, you're still quite beautiful!

Bystrouška:

[pɔt͡ʃkɛⁱ pɔt͡ʃkɛⁱ tɔ   sɪ pɔviːmɛ v‿ mɲɛsiːt͡sɪ   maːjɪ]

Počkej, počkej, to   si povíme   v   měsíci   máji.
Wait,   wait,   that we'll see in month   of May.

Wait, wait, we'll see in the month of May.

[pɔt͡ʃkɛⁱ pɔt͡ʃkɛⁱ tɔ   sɪ pɔviːmɛ v‿ mɲɛsiːt͡sɪ   maːjɪ]

Počkej, počkej, to   si povíme   v   měsíci   máji.
Wait,   wait,   that we'll see in month   of May.

Wait, wait, we'll see in the month of May.

Lišák:

[pɔtʃkaːm   pɔtʃkaːm   pɔtʃkaːm   pɔtʃkaːm]

Počkám,   počkám,   počkám,   počkám.
I'll wait,   I'll wait,   I'll wait,   I'll wait.

I'll wait, I'll wait, I'll wait, I'll wait.

Harašta: [12]see note

[gdɪʃ   ⁱsɛm jaː ʃɛl   ʔɔkɔlɔ   ɦaːja   zɛlɛnɛːɦɔ]

Když   jsem já šel   okolo   hája   zeleného,
When   I went   around   grove   green,

As I went around the green grove,

[natr̩ɦal   ⁱsɛm   lupɛɲiː   dɔ‿   ʃaːtka   biːlɛːɦɔ]

natrhal   jsem   lupení   do   šátka   bílého.
I gathered   leaves   to   kerchief   white.

I gathered leaves in my white kerchief.

Lišák:

[pɔtʃkaːm   pɔtʃkaːm   v‿ mɲɛsiːt͡sɪ   maːjɪ]

Počkám,   počkám   v   měsíci   máji,
I'll wait,   I'll wait   in   month   of May,

I'll wait, I'll wait in the month of May,

[pɔtʃkaːm   pɔtʃkaːm   ʔaʃ   sɪ tɔ pɔviːmɛ   v‿ mɲɛsiːt͡sɪ   maːjɪ]

počkám,   počkám,   až   si to povíme   v   měsíci   máji.
I'll wait,   I'll wait,   until - that we'll see in   month   of May.

I'll wait, I'll wait until we see in the month of May.

Bystrouška: Lišák:

[gdɔ tɔ tu   vřiːskaː]   [gdɔ tɔ tu   vřiːskaː]

Kdo to tu   vříská?   **Kdo to   tu   vříská?**
Who that there screams?   Who that there screams?

Who's screaming over there?   *Who's screaming over there?*

Bystrouška:

[ⁱd'ɪ   skɔvɛː   sɛ]

Jdi!   Skové   se!
Go!   Hide!

Go! Hide!

(Harašta se blíží s nůší plnou drůbeže.)
(Harašta approaches with a basket full of poultry.)

[prɔtʃ   bɪx   sɛ nɛpɔd'iːvala jakiː   tɔ   t͡ʃlɔvjɛk]

Proč   bych   se nepodívala,   jaký   to   člověk?
Why   would I   not see   what kind   that   man?

Why shouldn't I see what kind of man it is?

(Vyloží se proti Haraštovi.) (She lies out in the open facing Harašta.)

Harašta: [13]see note

[dɔnɛsu jaː fio dɔ ‿ lɔʒɛ gdɛ maː mɪlaː lɛʒiː]

Donesu já ho do lože, kde má milá leží.
Will take I it to bed, where my dear lies.

I'll take it to bed where my sweetheart is lying.

[ʔɔtɛvři mɪ maː mɪlaː]

Otevři mi, má milá,
Open to me, my sweetheart,

Open the door for me, my dear,

(Shlédne Bystroušku, postaví rychle nůši na zem.)
(He glimpses Bystrouška and quickly puts the basket on the ground.)

[nuːʃu duːlɛ fiaraʃtɔ fiaraʃtɔ ʃt͡ʃageːl dɔ ‿ rukɪ]

Nůšu důle! Harašto, Harašto! [14]Ščagél do ruky!
Basket down! Harašta, Harašta! Stick to hand!

Put the basket down! Harašta, Harašta! Pick up your rifle!

(Vytahuje z nůše pušku a skládá ji.)
(He pulls a rifle out of his basket and gets it ready.)

[fiuː na ‿ ɲu tɔ budɛ ʃtut͡s prɔ ‿ tɛrɪŋku]

Hú, na ňu! To bude štuc pro Terynku.
So, on her! That will be muff for Terynka.

Let's get her! It'll be a muff for Terynka.

Bystrouška:

[tɔʃ   tɪ   tak]

Tož,   ty   tak?
Then,   you   so?

So, you want this?

(Pustí se šourem přes cestu; poskakuje nemotorně, vleče se, jak by
nemohla na všechny čtyři.)
(She sets out slowly across the path; she hops clumsily, she drags herself as if she couldn't walk on all fours.)

(Harašta honí se za ní; míří a zase svěsí pušku podle toho, jak Bystr.
mu nadbíhá, neb se skrývá.)
(Harašta runs after her; he aims and again lowers the rifle accordingly as
Bystrouška outruns him or hides.)

[biːt   zabiːt   jɛn   prɔtɔ   ʒɛ   su   lɪʃka]

Bít,   zabít,   jen   proto,   že   su   liška!
To beat, to kill,   only   because   that   I am   vixen!

To beat, to kill, just because I'm a vixen!

[biːt   zabiːt   jɛn   prɔtɔ   ʒɛ   su   lɪʃka]

Bít,   zabít,   jen   proto,   že   [15]su   liška!
To beat, to kill,   only   because   that   I am   vixen!

To beat, to kill, just because I'm a vixen!

(Har. se pouští po svahu za Bystr.)
(Harašta sets out down the slope after Bystrouška.)

[biːt   zabiːt]

¹⁶**Bít,   zabít?**
To beat,   to kill?

To beat, to kill?

¹⁷<u>see note</u>
(Harašta klopýtá . . . a upadne) (Harašta trips . . . and falls)

Harašta: Bystrouška:

[raːnɪ   bɔʒiː]   [spravuⁱ sɪ   svuːˑⁱ   nɔs]

Rány   boží!   ¹⁸**Spravuj si   svůj   nos,**
Wounds   of God!   You tend to   your   nose,

Good heavens!   *You tend to your nose,*

[ʔa jaː   tvɔju   nuːʃu]

a   já   tvoju   nůšu!
and I   to your   basket!

and I to your basket!

(Utíká k nůši.) (She runs up to the basket.)

Harašta:

[ʔɔxɔxɔ]

Ochocho!
Ouch!

(Ohmatává si rozbitý nos.) (He feels his broken nose.)

[raːnɪ   bɔʒiː   t͡sɔ   jaː tɛrɪnt͡sɛ   ř̌ɛknu   ʔuvɪd'a   ju]

Rány   boží!   Co   já   Terynce   řeknu,   uvid̆a   ju!
Wounds of God! What I   to Terynka will say,   I will see   her!

Good heavens! What will I say to Terynka when I see her!

[ʔɔxɔxɔ   ʔɔxɔxɔ   t͡sɔ   jaː tɛrɪnt͡sɛ   ř̌ɛknu   ʔuvɪd'a   ju]

Ochocho! Ochocho! Co já Terynce   řeknu,   uvid̆a   ju!
Ouch!   Ouch!   What I   to Terynka will say, I will see her!

Ouch! Ouch! What will I say to Terynka when I see her!

[ʔant͡sɪjaːʃ   pɛkɛlnɛː   nadɛfinal   ju]

Anciáš   pekelné   nadehnal   ju!
Devil   infernal   drove   her!

The devil sent her!

(Vrací se těžce k nůši.) (With difficulty he goes back to the basket.)

Bystrouška:

[biːt   zabiːt]

Bít,   zabít,
To beat, to kill,

To beat, to kill,

(Z nůši peři jen lítá.) (Feathers from the basket are just streaming out.)

[jɛn prɔtɔ ʒɛ su lɪʃka]

jen proto, že su liška!
only because that I am vixen!

just because I'm a vixen!

[biːt zabiːt jɛn prɔtɔ ʒɛ su lɪʃka]

Bít, zabít, jen proto, že su liška!
To beat, to kill, only because that I am vixen!

To beat, to kill, just because I'm a vixen!

[biːt zabiːt jɛn prɔtɔ ʒɛ su lɪʃka]

Bít, zabít, jen proto, že su liška!
To beat, to kill, only because that I am vixen!

To beat, to kill, just because I'm a vixen!

(Harašta se zastaví v němém úžasu.) (Harašta stops, dumbfounded.)

[ʔɔdnɛsulɪ kuřaːtkɔ t͡sɔ tu plaːt͡ʃɛ t͡sɔ tu plaːt͡ʃɛ]

Odnesu-li kuřátko, co tu pláče, co [19]tu pláče?
I carry away-if chick, that here cries, that here cries?

How about if I carry off a chick that's crying here, that's crying here?

Harašta: (pln vzteku a hoře nazdařbůh míří a střelí do lišek)
(full of rage and sorrow, he randomly aims and shoots at the foxes)

[tɔtɔk   zdɛ]

Totok   zde?
This   there?

This one?

⊕ Rána Shot   ⊕ Rána Shot

(Lišky se rozběhnou v záplavě peří. Zmirající Bystr. zůstane ležet.)
(The foxes scatter in a flood of feathers. The dying Bystrouška remains
lying.)

Opona. Curtain.

Proměna   Scene change   [Act III, scene ii]

„U Pásků" v zahradě; na kuželně. Nezvyklé ticho.
"U Pásků" in the garden; in the bowling alley. Unusual silence.

Opona

Revírník: (K pí. Páskové, jež donáší pivo) (To Mrs. Pásková, who
brings the beer)

[ʔa gdɛ   ʔɔtɛt͡s   paːsɛk]

A   kde   otec   Pásek?
And where   innkeeper   Pásek?

And where's the innkeeper Pásek?

Paní Pásková:

[jɛ   v ‿ br̩ɲɛ   jɛ   pl̩nɔ   praːt͡sɛ]

Je	**v**	**Brně.**	**Je**	**plno**	**práce.**
He is	in	Brno.	It is	full	of work.

He's in Brno. There's so much work to do.

[liːt͡ʃiːmɛ   nɛɲiː   dɔ ‿ viːkladuː]

Líčíme . . .		**není**	**do**	**výkladů.**
We're whitewashing . . .	it's not	to	comments.

We're whitewashing . . . there's no time to talk.

(Odchází.) (She leaves.)

Revírník: (k zamlklému rechtorovi) (to the silent Schoolmaster)

[tɔʃ   ᶦdu   pɔ ‿ stɔpjɛ   lɪʃt͡ʃiː]

Tož	**jdu**	**po**	**stopě**	**liščí,**
Then	I go	along	footprints	vixen's,

Then I follow the vixen's footprints,

[ʔa   nandu   dɔːupjɛ   ʔɔpuʃtʼɛnɛː]

a	**nandu**	**doupě**	**opuštěné.**
and	I find	lair	abandoned.

and I find her lair abandoned.

[nɔ   rɾɛxtɔrku]

No,   rechtorku,
Well,   Rechtor,

Well, Schoolmaster,

[nɛuⁱdɛ   t'ɪ   pR̆etse̯ suxɛː jazɪk   lɪʃt͡ʃiː]

neujde   ti   přece   suché jazyk liščí.
it will not miss to you still   dry   tongue vixen's.

you'll soon have your dried vixen's tongue after all.

[viːʃ   ʒɛ   d'ɛlaː   nɛvɪd'ɪtɛlniːm]

Víš,   že   dělá   neviditelným?
Do you know   that   it makes invisible?

Do you know that it makes you invisible?

[In orchestra: (*vesele*) (*cheerfully*)]

[ʔɪ   mɛː   starɛː   ʃtut͡s   nɛuⁱdɛ]

I   mé   staré   štuc   neujde.
And   my   old woman muff   it will not miss.

And my old woman'll get her muff.

[ʃak   sɛ   t'ɪ   tɔ   zɦɔd'iː   rɛxtɔrku]

Šak   se   ti   to   zhodí,   rechtorku,
For sure   -   to you   it   will come in handy,   Schoolmaster,

For sure, it'll come in handy for you, Schoolmaster,

[ʔaʃ   pudɛʃ   na‿   naːmluvɪ   za‿   slunɛt͡ʃɲɪt͡sama]

až   pudeš   na   námluvy   za   slunečnicama.
when   you will go   for   courting   after   sunflowers.

when you go courting sunflowers.

Rechtor:

[tɔ   ʔuʃ   nɛ]

To   už   ne!
That   already   not!

Certainly not!

(Pí. Páková vstoupí) (Mrs. Pásek enters)
[slɛt͡ʃna   tɛrɪŋka   sɛ   zrɔvna   dnɛs   vdaːvaː]

Slečna   Terynka   se   zrovna   dnes   vdává.
Miss   Terynka   -   just   today   is getting married.

Miss Terynka's getting married this very day.

(Rechtor se obrátí ku plotu, zastíní si oči dlaní a dívá se kamsi přes okolní zahrádky.)
(The Schoolmaster turns toward the fence, shades his eyes with his palm, and looks somewhere across the neighboring garden.)

Paní Pásková:

[maː   nɔviː   ʃtuts   nɔviː   ʃtuts]

Má   nový   štuc.   Nový   štuc!
She has   new   muff.   New   muff!

She's got a new muff. A new muff!

Rechtor: (pro sebe) (to himself)

[snat   nɛvɪd'ɛl]

Snad   neviděl?
Maybe   he didn't see?

Maybe he didn't see me?

Revírník: (potřásá rechtorovi rukou) (he shakes the Schoolmaster's hand) (Rechtor se obrací k revírníkovi) (The Schoolmaster turns to the Forester)

[dɔ ‿ fɪrɔma   suxɛː   jakɔ   lɔːtʃ]

Do   hroma!   Suché,   jako   lóč
To   thunder!   Dry,   like   stick of kindling

Damn! Dry like a stick of kindling,

[ʔa   pŘɛtsɪ   s ‿ ʔɔka   krapɛtʃku   vɪpɔt'iː]

a   přeci   z   oka   krapečku   vypotí?
and   yet   from eye   little drop   he sweats?

and still he sheds a tear?

[ɲɪt͡s   kamaraːdɛ   dɔbřɛ jɛ   tʼɪ]

Nic,   kamaráde!   Dobře je   ti!
Nothing,   friend!   Well   is it to you!

It's nothing, my friend! You're doing well!

[t͡sɔ   bɪ sɪs   pɔt͡ʃal s ‿ takɔvɔu ʒɛnskɔu]

Co   by sis počal   s   takovou   ženskou?!
What   would you do   with such   woman?!

What would you do with a woman like her?!

[tɔ bɪ bɪl   pjɛknɛː kɔntrapuŋkt   latɪʼna tu   sxaːziː]

To   by byl   pěkné [20]kontrapunkt! [21]Latina tu   schází.
That would be nice   counterpoint! Latin here is missing.

That would be some counterpoint!   Latin is missing here.

(k pí. Páskové) (to Mrs. Pásek)
[jak   jɛ   mu   ʔasɪ   vɛ ‿ straːɲiː]

Jak   je   mu   asi   ve   [22]Stráni?
How   is it to him perhaps in   Stráň?

How's he doing, then, in Stráň?

Paní Pásková:

[psal   starɛːmu   tɛskɲiː]

Psal   starému.   Teskní ...
He wrote   to the old man.   He's homesick ...

He wrote to my husband. He's homesick ...

Revírník: (náhle) (all of a sudden)

[zaplat'iːm   ʔa   puːⁱdu]

Zaplatím   a   půjdu.
I'll pay   and   I'll go.

I'll pay and go.

Rechtor: (s podivením, měkce) (with wonder, gently)

[ʔa   kam   tak   br̥zɔ]

A   kam   tak   brzo?
And   to where so   early?

And where to so early?

(Rev. platí pí. Páskoví) (The Forester pays Mrs. Pásek)
Revírník:

[kam   dɔ ‿ lɛsa   ʔa   dɔm]

Kam?   Do   lesa   a   dom.
Where to?   To   forest   and   home.

Where to? To the forest and then home.

[lapaːtʃka ⁱsɛm nɛvzal s ‿ sɛbɔu bɔlɪjou fiɔ nɔʃkɪ]

Lapáčka jsem nevzal s sebou, ²³Bolijou ho nožky,
Lapák I didn't take with me, they hurt him legs,

I didn't take Lapák with me, his legs hurt him,

[pɔlɛfiaːvaː   jɛ starɛː rɛxtɔrku   jakɔ mɪ]

polehává,   je staré, rechtorku,   jako my.
he resorts to bed at times, he's old, Schoolmaster, like us.

he has to lie around, he's old, Schoolmaster, like us.

[jak   daːvnɔ   tɔmu   filɔupɔst'ɪ   ⁱsmɛ vɪvaːd'ɛlɪ]

Jak   dávno   tomu,   hlouposti   jsme vyváděli.
How   long ago   to it,   foolishness   we carried on.

How long it's been since we carried on like fools.

[ʔa   ftʃɪl   tʃlɔvjɛk jɛ   raːt gdɪʃ   ɲɛgdɛ   sɪ pR̆ɪtʃapiː]

A včil člověk je rád, když někde   si přičapí,
And now man is glad when somewhere he squats,

And now a man is glad when he can squat down somewhere,

[ʔa   nɛxt͡sɛ   sɛ   mu   ʔaɲɪ   fiɲɪ]

a   nechce   se   mu   ani   hni!
and   he doesn't want   -   to him   even   budge an inch!

and he doesn't even want to move at all!

(Odchází.) (He leaves.)

Opona (Proměna)   Curtain (Scene change)

[Act III, scene iii]

Opona.   Curtain.

Černý, suchý žleb jako v I. jednání. Slunce vysvitne po pršce.
Black, dry ravine like in Act I. The sun is shining again after rain.
(Revírník stoupá do stráně.) (The Forester is climbing up the hillside.)

Revírník: srdečně (heartily)   [24]see note

[nɛři:kal   ⁱsɛm   tɔ   malɔvani: jak   vɔja:t͡ʃɛk]

Neříkal	**jsem**	**to?!**	**Malovaný**	**jak**	**vojáček!**
Said	I	it?!	Painted	like	little soldier!

Didn't I say it?!   Painted like a little soldier!

[25]see note

[palɪt͡ʃka   kaʃtanɔva: jakɔ   d'ɛft͡ʃa:tkɔ]

Palička	**kaštanová,**	**jako**	**děvčátko.**
Cap	chestnut-colored,	like	little girl.

A chestnut-colored cap like a little girl.

(Hladí zdravý, štíhlý hřib.)
(He strokes a healthy, slender mushroom [boletus])

[In piano/vocal score, for the horns: s leskem 'with brilliance']

[26]see note

[jɛ   tɔ   pɔfiaːtka   t͡ʃɪ   pravda   pɔfiaːtka   t͡ʃɪ   pravda]

Je   to   pohádka   či   pravda? Pohádka   či   pravda?
Is   it   fairy tale   or   truth?   Fairy tale   or   truth?

Is it a fairy tale or real?   A fairy tale or real?

[kɔlɪk   jɛ tɔmu lɛt   t͡sɔ ⁱsmɛ kraːt͡ʃɛlɪ dva mlad'iː lɪdɛː]

Kolik   je tomu let,   co jsme kráčeli dva mladí lidé,
How many   is to it years, what we stepped two young people,

How many years is it since we two young people stepped here,

[ʔɔna   jak   jɛdlɪt͡ʃka   ʔɔn   jak   ʃɛriː   bɔr]

ona   jak   jedlička,   on   jak   šerý   bor?
she   like   little fir,   he   like   wide   pine wood?

she as straight as a little fir tree, he broad like pine wood?

[takeː   ⁱsmɛ   fɪřiːpkɪ   zbiːralɪ]

Také   jsme   hříbky   sbírali,
Also   we did   little mushrooms   collect,

Also, we picked little mushrooms;

[tuzɛ   pɔfimɔʒd'ɪlɪ   pɔʃlapalɪ]

tuze   pohmoždili,   pošlapali,
very much   we bruised,   we trampled,

we really bruised them, we trampled on them,

[prɔtɔʒɛ   prɔtɔʒɛ   prɔ ‿ laːsku   ⁱsmɛ nɛvɪdʼɛlɪ]

protože ... protože   pro   lásku   jsme   neviděli.
because ... because   for   love   we did not see.

because ... because of love we didn't see.

[tsɔ   fʃag   ɦubjɛnɛk]

Co   však   huběnek,
What   however   kisses,

But what kisses,

[tsɔ   fʃag   ɦubjɛnɛk   ⁱsmɛ   nazbiːralɪ]

co   však   huběnek   jsme   nasbírali!
what   however   kisses   we   gathered!

but what kisses we gathered!

[tɔ   bɪl   dɛn   pɔ ‿ naʃiː   svadbjɛ]

To   byl   den   po   naší   svatbě,
That   was   day   after   our   wedding,

That was the day after our wedding,

[27]see note

[bɔʒɛ   tɔ   bɪl   dɛn   pɔ ‿ naʃiː svadbjɛ]

bože   **to**   **byl**   **den**   **po**   **naší**   **svatbě!**
good Lord,   that   was   day   after   our   wedding!

good Lord, that was the day after our wedding!

(Přišel až k vrcholku; usedne, opře pušku o kolena.)
(He arrives at the top of the hill; he sits down, he rests his rifle on his knee.)

[gdɪbɪ   nɛ   mux]

Kdyby   **ne**   **much,**
If there were   no   flies,

If it weren't for the flies,

[t͡ʃlɔvjɛk   bɪ   f ‿ tu   mɪnutu   ʔusnul]

člověk   **by**   **v**   **tu**   **minutu**   **usnul . . .**
person   would   in   this   minute   fall asleep . . .

a person would fall asleep in a minute . . .

[ʔa   pR̝ɛt͡sɛ   su   raːt]

A   **přece**   **su**   **rád,**
And   yet   I am   glad,

And yet I'm glad

[gdɪʃ   k ‿ viːtʃerɔm   sluɲiːtʃkɔ   zabliːsknɛ]

když   **k**   **víčerom**   **sluníčko**   **zablýskne** . . .
when   toward   evening   little sun   will flash . . .

when toward evening the little sun flashes . . .

[jak   jɛ   lɛs   d'ɪvukrraːsniː]

Jak   **je**   **les**   **divukrásný!**
How   is   forest   spectacular!

How spectacular the forest is!

[ʔaʃ   rusalkɪ   pŘɪ'dou   zasɛ   dɔmuː]

Až   **rusalky**   **přijdou**   **zase**   **domů,**
Until   water nymphs   arrive   again   home,

When the water nymphs arrive back home

[dɔ ‿ sviːx   lɛtɲiːx   siːdɛl]

do   **svých**   **letních**   **sídel,**
to   their   summer   abode,

to their summer abode,

[pŘɪbjɛɦnou   f ‿ kɔʃɪlkaːx]

přiběhnou   **v** [28]**košilkách**
they will run   in   light robes

they will run up in their light robes

[ʔaʒ   zasɛ   pR̝ɪⁱdɛ   k‿ ɲɪm   kvjɛtɛn   ʔa   laːska]

až   zase   přijde   k   nim   květen   a   láska!
until   again   arrives   to   them   May   and   love!

until May and love will come again to them!

[viːtat   sɛ   budɔu]

Vítat   se   budou,
Welcome   one another   they will,

They will welcome one another

[sl̩zɛt   pɔɦinut'iːm   nad‿   zɦilɛdaːɲiːm]   ²⁹see note

slzet   pohnutím   nad   shledáním!
shed tears   from emotion   over   reunion!

and with emotion shed tears over their reunion!

[zas   rɔzd'ɛliː   ʃt'ɛst'iː   slatkɔu   rɔsɔu]

Zas   rozdělí   štěstí   sladkou   rosou
Again   they will spread   happiness   by sweet   dew

Again they will spread happiness by sweet dew

[dɔ ‿ t'ɪsiːt͡suː   kvjɛtuː]

do   tisíců   květů,
to   thousand   blossoms,

to a thousand blossoms,

[pɛtr̩kliːt͡ʃuː   lɛx   ʔa   sasanɛk]

petrklíčů,	**lech**	**a**	[30]**sasanek,**
primroses,	meadow peas	and	anemones,

primroses, meadow peas, and anemones,

[ʔa   lɪdɛː   budou   xɔd'ɪt   z ‿ fɪlavamɪ   sklɔpɛniːmɪ]

a	**lidé**	**budou**	**chodit**	**s**	**hlavami**	**sklopenými**
and	people	will	go	with	heads	cast down

and people will walk with their heads bowed low,

[ʔa   budɔu   xaːpat]

a	**budou**	**chápat,**
and	they will	grasp,

and they will understand

[ʒɛ   ʃlɔ   vuːkɔl   ɲɪx   natpɔzɛmskɛː   blaɦɔ]

že	**šlo**	**vůkol**	**nich**	**nadpozemské**	**blaho.**
that	it went	around	them	unearthly	bliss.

that around them has come an unearthly bliss.

(S úsměvem usíná. Rozestupuje se mlází. V pozadí vynoří se [31]jeřáb s obrázkem, sova, vážka a všechna zvířata z I. jed.)
(With a smile he falls asleep. The undergrowth spreads apart. In the background appear the [31]crane with the scene, the owl, the dragonfly, and all the animals from the first act.)

(Se nadzdvihne ve snu.) (He lifts himself in his dream.)

[ɦɔⁱ   ʔalɛ   nɛɲiː   tu   bɪstrouʃkɪ]

Hoj!	**Ale**	**není**	**tu**	**Bystroušky!**
Hey!	But	it's not	that	Bystrouška!

Hey! But it's not that Bystrouška!

(Malinká lištička přiběhne až k rev.)
(A tiny little vixen runs up to the Forester.)

[ɦilɛ   tu   jɛ   maliːt͡ʃkaː   rɔzmazlɛnaː]

Hle,	**tu**	**je!**	**Maličká**	**rozmazlená!**
Look,	here	she is!	Tiny	pampered!

Look, here she is! A tiny spoiled one!

[ʔuʃkliːbɛnaː jag   bɪ   maːmɲɛ   s ‿ ʔɔka   vɪpadla]

ušklíbená	**jak**	**by**	**mámě**	**z**	**oka**	**vypadla!**
grinning	how	she would	to mom	from	eye	appear!

grinning like the spitting image of her mother!

[pɔt͡ʃkɛː   tɛbɛ   sɪ   drapnu   jak   tvɔju   maːmu]

[32]**Počké,**	**tebe**	**si**	**drapnu,**	**jak**	**tvoju**	**mámu,**
Wait,	you	I will	grab,	like	your	mother,

Wait, I'll grab you like your mother,

[ʔalɛ   lɛːpɛ   sɪ   tʼɛ   vɪxɔvaːm]

ale   lépe   si   tě   vychovám
but   better   -   you   I will raise

but I will raise you better

[ʔabɪ   lɪdɛː   ʔɔ ‿ mɲɛ ʔa   ʔɔ ‿ tɔbjɛ   nɛpsalɪ]

aby   lidé   o   mně   a   o   tobě   nepsali
so that   people   about   me   and about you   won't write

so people won't write about me and about you

[v ‿ nɔvɪnaːx]

v   novinách.
in   newspapers.

in the newspapers.   [33]see note

(Nadzdvihuje se, rozpřáhne ruce, ale zachytí skokánka.)
(He gets up, he stretchs out his arms, but he catches a frog.)

(Zvířata se ze ztrnulosti probírají.) (The animals wake from their daze.)

[ʔɛx   tɪ   pɔtvɔrɔ   studɛnaː   gdɛ   sɛ   tu   bɛrɛʃ]

Eh,   ty   potvoro   studená,   kde   se   tu   bereš?
Eh,   you   bastard   cold,   where -   here you go?

Eh, you cold bastard, where did you come from?

Skokánek:

[tɔtɔk   nɛⁱsɛm   jaː   tɔtɔk   bɛlɪ   d'ɛdɔːʃɛk]

Totok   **nejsem**   **já,**   **totok**   **beli**   **dědóšek!**
This   am not   I,   this   was   grandpa!

I'm not that one, that was my grandpa!

[ʔɔɲɪ   mɲɛ   ʔɔ ‿ vaːs   vɛvɛvɛvɛ]

Oni   **mně**   **o**   **vás**   **veveveve,**
They   to me   about   you   t-t-t-t,

They talked to me about y-y-y-you,

[ʔɔɲɪ   ʔɔ ‿ vaːs   vɛvɛvɛklaːdalɪ]

oni   **o**   **vás**   **vevevekládali.**
they   about   you   t-t-talked.

they talked about y-y-you.

(Revírník ovi spadne v zapomenutí puška na zem.)
(The Forester drops his rifle to the ground in forgetfulness.) [34]see note

Opona. (zvolna padá)   **Curtain.** (it slowly falls)

Lišák caressing Bystrouška, one of the drawings by Stanislav Lolek (1873-1936) used in the original novel *Liška Bystrouška* (Těsnohlídek 1995, 189). Reprinted with the permission of Ctibor Lolek.

Appendix A

Pronunciation Checklist

The following is a final Check/Czech list to guard against common Anglicisms in Czech lyric pronunciation.

(1) Are the [a] and other vowels bright, like Italian, along with Italianate unaspirated, forward consonants? They should be!

(2) Are all *e*'s—*é, e, ě*—open [ɛ]? Make sure, especially, that all final *e*'s are open.

(3) Make sure that every *mě* is pronounced [mɲɛ]. This is one of the few nonphonetic issues in Czech, and it is very important.

(4) Is every *d, n,* and *t* softened when it occurs before an *i/í* (except for foreign-derived words)? Remember "I Did, Didn't I?" in chapter 2 of *Singing in Czech* (Cheek 2001, 44–45)!

(5) Are all vocalic *r*'s rolled long enough?

(6) Is every [ɦ] voiced? In consonant clusters, approach them as grace notes. Also, make sure [ɦ] and [x] are two very different sounds!

(7) Remember that final *h* is pronounced [x].

(8) Make sure that *s* between vowels is pronounced [s], and *not* [z]. Do not confuse this with Italian and French pronunciation.

(9) Make sure not to carry over German rules into Czech: e.g., initial *sl* is sung [sl], and not [ʃl]. Czech [x] is more forward than German.

183

(10) Look carefully at the rhythm and stress, to make sure that words begin as notated on a strong beat.

(11) Where the music allows for it, *bend* rhythms to accommodate long vowels. This is an important part of Czech inflection, and Janáček often allows for it.

(12) Make sure that the Czech diphthong *ou* is *not* pronounced as in the English word *ouch*.

(13) Are you observing the glottals? These come naturally to Czech singers, and they must be observed.

(14) Do not confuse the *čárka* sign with the *háček*: the words *mé, mne,* and *mě* are all pronounced differently: [mɛː], [mnɛ], and [mɲɛ].

Appendix B

Recordings

Helena Tattermuschová, Bystrouška
Zdeněk Kroupa, Revírník
Eva Zikmundová, Lišák
Prague National Theatre Chorus and Orchestra
Bohumil Gregor, conductor
Recorded 1970
Supraphon, no. 3071-2
2 CD's AAD

Magdaléna Hajóssyová, Bystrouška
Richard Novák, Revírník
Gabriela Beňačková-Čápová, Lišák
Kühn Children's Chorus
Czech Philharmonic Chorus and Orchestra
Václav Neumann, conductor
Recorded 1979-1980
Supraphon, no. 103471-2
2 CD's AAD

Lucia Popp, Bystrouška
Dalibor Jedlička, Revírník
Eva Randová, Lišák
Vienna Philharmonic
Sir Charles Mackerras, conductor
Recorded 1981
London Classics, no. 417129
2 CD's DDD

Lívia Ághová, Bystrouška
Ivan Kusnjer, Revírník
Annette Jahns, Lišák
Venice Teatro la Fenice Orchestra and Chorus
Zoltán Peskó, conductor
Recorded 1999
Mondo Musica, no. 22251
2 CD's DDD

In English:

Lilian Watson, Vixen
Thomas Allen, Forester
Diana Montague, Fox
Chorus and Orchestra of the Royal Opera House, Convent Garden
Simon Rattle, conductor
Recorded 1990
EMI, no. 7542122
2 CD's DDD

Video (DVD widescreen)

Eva Jenis, Bystrouška
Thomas Allen, Revírník
Hana Minutillo, Lišák
Orchestre de Paris
Sir Charles Mackerras, conductor
Brian Large, video director
Nicholas Hytner, stage director
Recorded live 1995
Arthaus Musik 100240
ASIN: B00005UDFM (Europe, Asia)
ASIN: B00000JN2W (USA)

Notes

Introduction

1. He committed suicide in 1928 in an office of the *Lidové noviny* (Tyrrell 1998, 218). For background in English on Těsnohlídek and Janáček's opera, see the afterword by Robert Jones in *The Cunning Little Vixen* (Těsnohlídek 1985, 167–86).

2. It was performed by bass Arnold Flögl (1885–1950), who had premiered the role of the Forester in Brno, and conductor František Neumann (1874–1929), who also had conducted the premiere (Tyrrell 1998, 238).

3. Líšeň is a part of Brno, the largest city of Moravia.

4. Many thanks to Professor Zdenka Brodská for clarifying this information, and for tracking down the explanation of *farář*, which follows.

5. The correct word is *Lištičky*. *Liščičky* is incorrect.

Act I

Scene i

1. The piano/vocal score has *bouřku*, which is "standard" Czech. Both the orchestral score and the original novel (Těsnohlídek 1995, 13) have the correct Moravian dialect, *bóřku*.

2. The orchestral score has *Spalehnu*, incorrect.

3. A bladder-nut is a shrub or small tree with white or pink flowers and bladderlike seed pods, from the genus *Staphylea*.

4. Be prepared to sing [svadɛbɲiː], a more formal delivery of this word, if the conductor requires it (Cheek 2001, 99). In the last scene,

the Forester again reminisces about the day after his wedding, but in a much deeper sense. There he speaks with insight as his life comes full circle.

5. Although both the orchestral and piano/vocal scores have *zmatrovaný*, perfectly correct "standard" Czech, the original novel has the Moravian *zmatrované*, more correct in this context (Těsnohlídek 1995, 13).

6. Similarly, *moje* is correct "standard" Czech and is printed in both the piano/vocal and orchestral scores. However, dialect is *moja*, and it occurs in the novel (Těsnohlídek 1995, 13). *This is one of very few recommended word changes.*

7. See "Characters" in the introduction for the distinction between a *myslivec* [gamekeeper], a *lovec* [hunter], and a *revírník* [forester].

8. Although *kmotřenka* is related to the word *kmotra* [grandmother], it occurs here as a village form of address. The orchestral score has *kmotřenko*, the vocative form of the word, which can be sung instead—both are correct.

9. At the *Meno mosso*, four measures before the *Tempo valčíku*, the metronome marking of 72 in the piano/vocal score is incorrect. The indication of 56 in the orchestral score is the correct one.

10. In the original Těsnohlídek, the Komár's exclamation is in response to seeing the sleeping Revírník. In the novel, he then lands on the Forester's nose and bites him. In the novel, and in Janáček's version, the Komár becomes drunk because he drinks the blood of the drunken Forester (Těsnohlídek 1995, 16–17).

11. *Malá* means *small*; *malinká* means *very small* and "cute," as well. Janáček uses both words to describe the baby Bystrouška.

12. The Komár can sing *když hřmělo* after the orchestra finishes.

13. Hold *jí* a little longer than an eighth.

14. This mild exclamation in pure Moravian dialect appears throughout the original story as one word (Těsnohlídek 1995, 5, 21, etc.). Depending on one's locale, the translation could be *darn!*, *shoot!*, *sheesh!*, *yikes!*, *gadzooks!*, etc. The singer can enter after the orchestra here.

15. The piano/vocal score is missing an *a tempo* in the third measure after Rehearsal 15. It comes after the *accelerando* on the B–C-sharp.

Act I, scene ii

16. A *myslivna* is a hunting lodge where the Forester lives. *Jezerská* is an adjective meaning *lake*. The Forester has named his house *Jezerská myslivna*, translated as *Lake Lodge*. There may or may not be a lake in the vicinity.

17. At Rehearsal 1 the dynamics in the orchestral score are the correct ones. They should be reversed in the piano/vocal score to *f* and *p*. The same holds true for Rehearsal 3.

18. Sing the *u* right after going to the second pitch.

19. The rhythm for these two words is different in the orchestral score from the piano/vocal score. The one in the orchestral score makes much more sense and should be used:

20. Lapák is the only character to speak in more formal standard Czech instead of in Moravian dialect. Perhaps this is because he has dedicated himself to art. The original Těsnohlídek actually has Lapák, a dachshund, speaking very little—only two short sentences (Těsnohlídek 1995, 35, 92). Those, too, are in standard Czech.

21. Try singing *Ou!* three times, one for each quarter note, even though only one is marked in both scores. Also, move quickly to the *u*—it sounds more like a dog howling.

22. *Oddat* means *to marry; oddat se* means *to devote oneself to*. Lapák foregoes love-making for art.

23. The original Těsnohlídek has the starling misbehaving in only one beech tree, *buku* (Těsnohlídek 1995, 32). Both the orchestral and piano/vocal scores have the plural, *buků*.

24. The *kroužek* [little circle] is missing in the orchestral score in the word *ořechů*.

25. Janáček has *ňáký* in the piano/vocal score, *ň'áký* in the orchestral score, and Těsnohlídek has *nějáké* (Těsnohlídek 1995, 38). Most idiomatic is *ňáké*.

26. A *ščagel* is dialect for a piece of dry twig or a stick (Těsnohlídek 1995, 211).

27. Whereas the orchestral score has the standard Czech *udeřil's* (= *udeřil jsi*), both the piano/vocal score and Těsnohlídek have *uderil's* (Těsnohlídek 1995, 39), without the *háček* over the *r*. *Uderil's* is the correct word for this colloquial outcry. In Act II, just before Rehearsal 57, both scores have the correct dialect: *uder* and *uderil*.

28. The *háček* in the piano/vocal score is missing. The orchestral score and Těsnohlídek (Těsnohlídek 1995, 39) correctly have *mně*.

29. The orchestral score has the wrong word, *savazí*. The piano/vocal score and the original have the correct word, *zavazí* (Těsnohlídek 1995, 42).

30. The scores have *ji*, but Těsnohlídek has *ju*, Moravian dialect (Těsnohlídek 1995, 42). The National Theatre in Prague also changed this to *ju* in its 1995 production.

31. Sing *u* immediately on the second eighth note, instead of just after moving to the second eighth. The emotion here calls for more than a normal diphthong!

32. Neither score indicates this, but it must be so.

33. The love motive is hinted at while Bystrouška dreams of being a girl.

34. *Trpět* means *to suffer*, and *trp* is the imperative. The way the hen sings it, it sounds like a chicken—go immediately to the rolled *r*, every time.

35. The chickens use the dialect word *kohóta*, and Bystrouška uses the standard Czech word *kohouta*, but both are really interchangeable.

36. *You see!*, as in *Eureka!*

37. This phrase should be sung very *legato*—this is why *než* is pronounced [nɛʒ] instead of [nɛʃ].

38. Sing the *u* of *Ou?* on the last eighth note.

39. On the first *Ou?*, sing the *u* on the D-sharp, as before. On the second *Ou?*, sing three *u*'s, one on each of the accented B's.

40. Although the scores have *starej*, the correct dialect is *staré*, which is how it appears in the original (Těsnohlídek 1995, 51).

41. There should be a fermata just before the double bar, on the singer's tied G. The singer and orchestra then come in together on *zastřel*, as written, but the tempo is slower, not ♩ = ♪., but ♪= ♪instead.

42. The *Più mosso* should probably start here at the beginning of the $\frac{2}{4}$ measure, rather than at Rehearsal 26.

43. Common practice here is for the orchestra to play up to the double bar—up to Rehearsal 26—and stop; the singer sings *Nebo já tebe!* alone; and the orchestra repeats the bar before Rehearsal 26 and continues as written.

Act II

Scene i

1. Sing the long vowel of *blechatá* longer than written, carrying it over the bar line.

2. Try the second phrase freer and a little slower than the first phrase.

3. Bystrouška does not bother to use the formal *you* to address the badger, as she deems him unworthy of respect. Formal would be *máte*, as opposed to the informal *máš*.

4. It is such toil for the badger to speak that he sweats.

5. Bystrouška is addressing the animals around the forest with *podívéte*.

6. The spelling should be *chlámat̆*.

7. Bystrouška has *zhnilé* and the Lesní havět' have *shnilé*, but the two words are pronounced exactly the same and mean the same thing.

8. This is a perfect example of Janáček's "Brno" style of going to the end of the phrase at *kluĉes*, abruptly stopping, breathing, and then starting the next phrase. The orchestra has to accommodate too, abruptly stopping before Rehearsal 6.

Act II, scene ii

9. The name of the inn is *u Pásků*, which means *at Pásek's*.

10. Not mentioned in the original Těsnohlídek, *Stráň* literally refers to the section of a hill part way up the side. Since the word is capitalized it can be the name of a village, a place in a forest or meadow, or the name of an inn or lodge. Because of the association between the Badger and the Pastor, who enters the scene "with the Badger's appearance," the line about things being better in Stráň could have two connotations—one for the Badger, who will be better off in his new home on the side of a hill, and one for the Pastor, who will move to a place that carries the name *Stráň*.

11. In creating this folksong-like passage, Janáček chose seven of Těsnohlídek's submission of fourteen lines for the libretto. Besides the original novel, this was Těsnohlídek's only contribution to the libretto. Note the intervals of the love motive here, up a perfect fourth and up a major second. The actual pitches of Janáček's love motive come at the words *na světě tratí*, A-flat to D-flat to E-flat. The motive goes back-

wards at *se stárla*, and *je lysý*, where the Forester says that the former lovers have grown old. Later, at *Veronika*, the Forester sings her name with accents and doesn't quite finish the motive, really irritating the Schoolmaster.

12. Make *–dřín* a little longer, *je* a little shorter. Play with the words here as the Forester makes a jab at the Schoolmaster's waning sexual prowess.

13. Note that the *n* in *Veronika* is not soft even though there is an *i* after it. This holds true for almost all Czech words of foreign origin, like the name *Veronika*. *Verunka*, used earlier, is a diminutive of *Veronika*.

14. Although both *potvora* and *bestie* are both translated as *bitch*, the word *bestie* is stronger than *potvora*. *Potvora* translates nowadays more like the word *creature*, but its meaning was stronger around the year 1920.

15. Rather than have the Pastor and Forester sing over one another, the Pastor should sing his line first, immediately followed by the Forester's "Kdyby to byla . . . " The orchestra simply repeats its two measures (repeat measures 4 and 5 of the Allegro).

16. Note that the *t* is soft in the word *latina*, following the *ti* rule, even though it is a foreign-derived word.

17. An *ostrývka* was a ladder made from only one pole.

18. The piano/vocal score has *kostrbatý*, but the correct Moravian is *kostrbaté*.

19. The orchestra plays the love motive right after *nežď'áráli* (with the same pitches as the original, enharmonically: G-sharp, C-sharp, D-sharp). The motive returns down a half-step at Rehearsal 19 and is then swept into the next four measures of the Allegro by the clarinet and bassoon, in an altered form, as the Schoolmaster rushes off.

20. Janáček added this chorus at the insistence of Max Brod to parallel the preceding scene with the Badger. Although Janáček agreed with Brod on this issue, and although it certainly makes the parallel much clearer, these two measures of chorus are usually cut in Czech productions of the opera. In this case, the orchestra plays the one measure with the trill and cuts the repeated measure.

21. *Šňupec* is literally a kind of snuff.

22. In the original Těsnohlídek, the Forester suspects right away that the Schoolmaster is not leaving them for sleep but because a woman is waiting for him. He then plunges into a diatribe against women (Těsnohlídek 1995, 69-70). The Schoolmaster is a Judas because he betrays the other men in the inn by not telling them that he has

a woman on his mind, and for deserting them. At this time and place in history men spent most of their time with other men, except those who were newlyweds. Jews often owned inns, so possibly the Forester is saying that the Schoolmaster would rather give himself over to a woman than to the innkeeper and his male comrades.

23. The Forester quotes Genesis 3:19: "By the sweat of your face you will eat bread, till you return to the ground, because from it you were taken; for you are dust, and to dust you shall return." (Scripture taken from the New American Standard Bible. Copyright 1960, 1962, 1963, 1968, 1971, 1972, 1973, 1975, 1977, 1995 by The Lockman Foundation. Used by permission.)

Act II, scene iii

24. Note that the d is not soft in the word mordié.

25. At this point in the original story, ". . . he sighed ardently and the expert musician rang in the Schoolmaster" (Těsnohlídek 1995, 73). All schoolmasters were musicians—it was an official requirement that they pass an exam in music and play the violin. Here, the Schoolmaster hears the slight rustling of the sunflower and thinks that he is hearing music.

26. A flagioletto is a small flute-like instrument with a mouthpiece, held vertically. Is this what the Schoolmaster is talking about?

27. At this point in the original, ". . . he moaned softly and with agitation his fingers grasped the stick to position it like the neck of his beloved bass" (Těsnohlídek 1995, 73).

28. Throughout his address to Terynka, the Schoolmaster uses the formal form of you, rather than the intimate form, highlighting his idealization of her.

29. In the original, the Schoolmaster says "For twenty-five years I've waited for you. . ." in between these two lines (Těsnohlídek 1995, 74).

30. Note that, as in the original, the Schoolmaster does not say "my fate is in your hands"—he is definitely drunk (Těsnohlídek 1995, 74)!

31. This line is usually sung after the orchestra.

32. At this point in the original, Těsnohlídek clearly says that she is pregnant by the butcher's apprentice (Těsnohlídek 1995, 82). The Pastor was blamed for it simply because he was so religious. Panáček means young priest, but here it could mean a seminarian, someone in theology school studying to be a priest. The Pastor did just say he was a young student.

33. These lines are said with irony—the Pastor compares her to the lovely catkin on a pussy willow; she pretended to be innocent, and also

she did not defend the Pastor's innocence.

34. Greek for "Remember to be a good man," the same line the Pastor said in Czech earlier while trying to remember its source. Note that *einai* is pronounced with four syllables. Note, too, the Czech pronunciation of *memnesthó* and *agathos*—here the *h* is silent, as in similar Greek words spelled in Czech with an *h*, such as *Pythagoras*, pronounced [pɪtagɔras].

35. *Anabasis* is Greek for *long journey*. Těsnohlídek and Janáček both have all short vowels, but the word is pronounced *Anabáze*. Xenofon was a Greek historian who lived c. 430-c. 355 B.C. He wrote about Socrates, among others. Many Czechs are familiar with the Czech expression *To byla ale Anabáse*, "That was quite an ordeal."

36. The *čárka* is missing in the piano/vocal score on the word *kujóne*.

37. The *riten.* and *Meno mosso* are usually not observed here.

Act II, scene iv

38. Note the love motive in the chorus and orchestra. The exact pitches, A-flat to D-flat to E-flat, occur starting at the *Più mosso*. Other occurrences in the orchestra are seven measures after Rehearsal 47, nine and ten measures after Rehearsal 47, and ten and eleven measures after Rehearsal 48. Transposed occurences are at Rehearsal 48, and the third and fourth measures after Rehearsal 50, as well as Rehearsal 45.

39. Note the strong, expressive [s] in *hezké* both times.

40. Like a gentleman, the Fox addresses Bystrouška with the formal *you* (using *jste* instead of *jsi*).

41. Saying *ne-e* instead of *ne* for *no* can show nervousness, embarrassment, or playfulness. Těsnohlídek writes this typical Moravian utterance sometimes as *néé* (Těsnohlídek 1995, 179–80), sometimes as *neé* (Těsnohlídek 1995, 186), sometimes as *nee* (Těsnohlídek 1995, 188), and sometimes with the "standard" *ne* (Těsnohlídek 1995, 182—*Kouříte snad? Ještě ne*, where Janáček writes *nee*.) Janáček writes *nee* or *neé*, but always uses two equal short notes. He never writes *néé*. The most idiomatic is the pronunciation *neé*, making the second vowel slightly longer than the first. Doing this every time throughout the opera would sound the most authentic.

42. The word *hnízdijou* should have a long *í*. *Ftáčci* is either dialect for *ptáčci* or more likely romantic baby talk.

43. Not standard Czech, *lefko* is probably romantic baby talk for

lehko rather than dialect.

44. Note the strong, expressive [s] in *laskavé*.

45. Note how Janáček marks both *tlumeně* [quietly] and *mf* at the same time! Try a loud whisper.

46. Bystrouška uses the informal *you* here, not deigning to give the Forester any respect.

47. The orchestra plays two phrases of the love motive, transposed, under the Fox's next line.

48. *Dozajista* is one word.

49. This is a perfect example of Janáček's *sčasovka*. Three measures earlier, at Rehearsal 61, Janáček sets up a rhythmic pattern in the bass which should not change when Bystrouška enters, despite the triplets. So, the effect is that the tempo is suddenly slower—the singer will·sense the new tempo by listening to the two sixteenth-notes in the treble, C and D, that immediately precede her entrance.

50. The eighth-notes on *doprovázel* are the same length as the preceding sixteenths on *aby*.

51. The eighth-note triplets in the orchestra are the same length as the preceding sixteenth-note triplets. Hold the high B-flat a little on *ideál* and enjoy the *quarter*-note triplet on *moderní*.

52. *Ruku líbám* is a very formal salutation and is not necessarily literal.

53. *Co je* should be two words in the score.

54. Someone who is *k světu* in Czech is either *pretty* or *capable*, or both.

55. Not aware that Lišák has returned, Bystrouška talks of him with the intimate *you*. She returns to the formal *you* in her next line.

56. *Chi chi* can be flirtatious or nervous. Related is the verb *chichtat se* "to giggle; to snicker."

57. It is common to sing the high B-flat for five beats, or even six, and then sing *Vy* just after the four chords in the strings. (Try learning *Vy*'s G-flat from the lower pitch of the chords, from the A-flat.)

58. Now Lišák switches to the intimate *you*.

59. *Odjakživa* is one word.

60. *Mě* in the score should be changed to *mne* both times.

61. *Včílka* is a misprint in the score.

62. Lišák uses an old literary form of *psát* "to write," adding elegance to his delivery.

63. An exception to the rule of pronouncing a glottal after *ne*: sing *neutíké* without a glottal, urgently but gently.

64. Stretch out a little the words *Aji já bych radost˘ou*, obviously more on the high A-sharp, and roll the *r* expressively.

65. It is traditional to hold the high B-flat for two beats (or even four beats) on *Chceš*.

66. See note 41.

67. The love motive blossoms here on the Woodpecker's line: A-flat, D-flat, E-flat.

68. The off-stage chorus begins here by singing the love motive, A-flat, D-flat, E-flat.

69. Take a breathe after *tentononc*. If another breathe is absolutely necessary, take another one after *si*.

70. At the *Allegro*, the piano/vocal score marks the half note at 104, whereas the orchestral score marks the quarter note at 104. The piano/vocal score is correct.

Act III

Scene i

1. Janáček introduces a Moravian folksong here. The words of the first verse were quoted in the original novel (Těsnohlídek 1995, 155).

2. The Revírník can sing here after the orchestra.

3. The word *tož* may be missing in the piano/vocal score.

4. *Ostudǔ* in the piano/vocal score is a misprint.

5. Here *macek* refers to a large, plump hare. (*Macka* is merely a different grammatical form of the word *macek*.) The word *macek* is often used as a name for a huge tomcat. It may also denote a plump animal or even a chubby child.

6. The spelling *liščičky* is incorrect. It should be *lištičky*. The Fox Cubs' folk text comes from the best known of all collections of Czech folksongs, Erben's *Czech Folksongs and Nursery Rhymes* (Tyrrell 1992, 285).

7. *Tábor* is a city in southern Bohemia, about 90 kilometers south of Prague. It was founded in 1420 on the site of a former Přemyslid settlement by a group of Hussites who set out on their battles from there. Mount Tabor has religious significance in both the Old Testament and—as the setting for Christ's transfiguration—in the New Testament (thus the choice of the Czech town's name for the religious Hussites).

8. *Zázvoru* and *bramborů* should exchange places in the scores because the line about *koření* [spices] belongs with *zázvoru* [ginger].

9. See note 41 for Act II, sc. iv.

10. Note *řet'az*, not *řetaz*.

11. The orchestral score marks a crescendo above the voice; the piano/vocal score has a diminuendo.

12. Harašta sings to a well-known folk text, set to Janáček's tune (Tyrrell 1992, 285).

13. The orchestral score has *na jevišti* [on the stage]—Harašta's previous lines were sung off-stage.

14. The *e* in *ščagél* should be long.

15. The piano/vocal score may have *sa*, a misprint.

16. The orchestral score has a different rhythm from the piano/vocal score. The piano/vocal score makes better sense for the inflection.

17. The orchestral score is marked *Allegro* at the first ¾ measure.

18. Bystrouška's line should come *after* Harašta's *Rány boží!*, not before. The orchestra simply holds its fermata trill until she is finished.

19. The piano/vocal score may repeat with *to*, a misprint.

Act III, scene ii

20. Remember that the Schoolmaster is a musician.

21. Referring to the Pastor.

22. See the opening of Act II, sc. ii, and the corresponding note 10.

23. These words can be sung more freely than notated by starting them a little sooner than written.

Act III, scene iii

24. This scene, the "Forester's Farewell," was performed at Janáček's memorial service in 1928.

25. In these two lines, the Forester speaks of the mushroom. Mushroom picking is still a national pastime in the Czech Republic. The *hřib* is edible and has a round-shaped cap. Most Eastern Europeans would immediately recognize this shape, as opposed to the poisonous toadstool of this part of the world that has a more conical-shaped cap with a "skirt." Colorful varieties and dots are also warning signs of the nonedible toadstool. Be sure to lengthen the long vowels in this section.

26. At Rehearsal 48, the piano/vocal score and orchestral score differ. The orchestral score should be followed. In the piano/vocal

score, play the first two measures of Rehearsal 48 three times; then, play the next measure; then, cut the next two measures; then, play the remaining two measures before the *Andante*.

27. In the very first scene of the opera, the Forester also remembers the day after his wedding, albeit in a much less contemplative context. The opera truly comes full circle.

28. A *košulka* is a linen top or shirt with sleeves. It was very long and so was often worn as a nightshirt.

29. Note the pronunciation of the word *shledáním*. The Moravian pronunciation of words beginning with *sh-* differs from the Bohemian. Moravian follows the usual rules of assimilation, voicing the *s* to [z]. Bohemian pronunciation would be [sxlɛdaːɲiːm], unvoicing the *h*. See Cheek 2001, 98–99.

30. After the word *sasanek* is an appropriate moment for an abrupt, unprepared lift, typical of Janáček, as the dynamic changes from *f* to *p*, and the singer takes a breath.

31. The crane is mentioned here for the first time in the opera. It might be argued that *crane* here could refer to the stage machinery that sets the scenery into place, since, like English, Czech *jeřáb* can denote both the bird and the machine. However, such an unwieldly machine is highly unlikely to be used to move scenery! So, seemingly for variety, Janáček introduces a new bird at the end of the opera.

32. The orchestral score has standard Czech, *počkej* (also used previously in the opera). The piano/vocal score is better here with the dialect, *počké*. The spelling *počkě* (with *ě*) was a misreading in the author's *Singing in Czech* (Cheek 2001, 288).

33. This refers, of course, to the original story of *Liška Bystrouška* published in the Brno *Lidové noviny* newspaper.

34. The love motive, A-flat to D-flat to E-flat, blossoms sixteen measures from the end in the horns. It had been hinted at, anticipated, and even played in veiled forms through the many rising perfect fourths throughout the final scene. Note, too, how above the love motive appears Bystrouška's melody from Act III, sc. i, Rehearsal 22, when she sings *to si povíme v měsíci máji* [we'll see in the month of May]. The final chord in the bass of the piano/vocal score should be only a quarter note in length.

References

Beckerman, Michael, and Bauer, Glen, editors. 1995. *Janáček and Czech music*. Stuyvesant: Pendragon Press.

Cheek, Timothy. 2001. *Singing in Czech: A guide to Czech lyric diction and vocal repertoire*, with a foreword by Sir Charles Mackerras. Lanham, Md.: Scarecrow Press.

Janáček, Leoš. 1924. *Příhody lišky Bystroušky* [The adventures of the vixen Bystrouška]. Orchestral score UE 7566. Vienna: Universal Edition.

———. 1925. *Příhody lišky Bystroušky* [The adventures of the vixen Bystrouška]. Piano/vocal score UE 7564, 2nd ed. (listed as 1924, however; with Czech and German). Vienna: Universal Edition.

Simeone, Nigel. 1991. *The first editions of Leoš Janáček*. Tutzing: Hans Schneider.

Simeone, Nigel, John Tyrrell, and Alena Němcová. 1997. *Janáček's works, a catalogue of the music and writings of Leoš Janáček*. Oxford: Clarendon Press.

Těsnohlídek, Rudolf. 1995. *Liška Bystrouška* [The vixen Bystrouška]. Illustrations by Stanislav Lolek. Prague: Bystrov a synové.

———. 1985. *The Cunning Little Vixen*. Translated by Tatiana Firkusny, Maritza Morgan, and Robert T. Jones. Afterword by Robert T. Jones. Illustrations by Maurice Sendak. New York: Farrar, Straus and Giroux.

Tyrrell, John. 1992. *Janáček's operas: A documentary account*. London: Faber and Faber.

———, ed. and trans. 1994. *Intimate letters: Leoš Janáček to Kamila Stösslová*. Princeton, N. J.: Princeton University Press.

———, ed. and trans. 1998. *My life with Janáček: The memoirs of Zdenka Janáčková*. London: Faber and Faber.

Vogel, Jaroslav. 1997. *Leoš Janáček*. Prague: Academia.

Zemanová, Mirka, ed. and trans. 1989. *Janáček's uncollected essays on music*. New York: Marion Boyars Publishers.

Index

About the Author

Pianist and vocal coach Timothy Cheek is assistant professor of performing arts at the University of Michigan School of Music in Ann Arbor, where he serves as music director of Opera Workshop, professor of lyric diction, diction coach for the University of Michigan Opera Theater, and associate faculty for the university's Center for Russian and East European Studies. He also serves on the faculty of the university's spring program in Florence, Italy, as pianist and coach, and together with colleague Martin Katz he has established and teaches a course in Slavic vocal literature at the University of Michigan. In addition, Cheek is on the international advisory board of the Kaprálová Society. His studies include a doctorate in piano accompanying and chamber music with famed pianist Martin Katz, and degrees in piano performance from the University of Texas and the Oberlin College Conservatory of Music. An active collaborative pianist, Dr. Cheek has performed recitals throughout thirteen countries on three continents, as well as on television and on worldwide radio broadcasts. A champion of the works of Czech composer Vítězslava Kaprálová (1915–40), he performed the world premieres of her song cycle *Jiskry z popele* in 2002 and the song "Leden" in 2003, and he is at work with Supraphon records to record the songs of Kaprálová with noted soprano Dana Burešová. His work with opera companies includes the Santa Fe Opera, the Michigan Opera Theater, and the Israel Vocal Arts Institute. Dr. Cheek was the recipient of a Fulbright Award to study as an opera coach apprentice at the Teatro Comunale in Florence, Italy, under conductors Bruno Bartoletti, Gianandrea Gavazzeni, and Zubin Mehta. He was also an apprentice of Czech opera at the National Theatre in Prague under noted Czech conductor Bohumil Gregor, and received an award from the International Research and Exchanges Board in Washington, D.C., for research on Czech lyric pronunciation. In addition to the "standard" repertoire, Dr. Cheek continues to coach and perform Czech vocal literature internationally. His book *Singing in Czech: A Guide to Czech Lyric Diction and Vocal Repertoire*, with a foreword by Sir Charles Mackerras, is published by Scarecrow Press.

Inquiries about supertitles, comments, or queries can be sent to:

timcheek@hotmail.com